Outwitting your Alcoholic

AN IDYLL ARBOR PERSONAL HEALTH BOOK

Outwitting your Alcoholic

Exploring and escaping from the strange world of alcoholism

Kenneth A. Lucas

Published and Distributed by

Idyll Arbor, Inc.

PO Box 720, Ravensdale, WA 98051 (425) 432-3231

Cover design by Pat Kenny.

Author's photograph by Mike Paulson.
"Channel" reprinted with permission of Story Line Press from
The Evening Light, by Floyd Skloot. © Copyright 1998 Story Line Press.

Idyll Arbor, Inc. editor Thomas M. Blaschko.

© Copyright 1998 by Idyll Arbor, Inc.

Library of Congress Cataloging-in-Publication Data

Lucas, Kenneth, 1946-
    Outwitting your alcoholic : exploring and escaping from the strange world of alcoholism / Kenneth Lucas.
            p.   cm.
    Includes bibliographical references and index.
    ISBN 1-882883-38-1 (alk. paper)
    1. Alcoholics--Family relationships. 2. Alcoholics' spouses. 3. Alcoholism. 4. Alcoholism--Treatment.   I. Title.
    HV5132.L83 1998
    362.292'3--dc21   98-17877
                                                                              CIP

ISBN 1-882883-38-1

ಶ

In time the fork my life took
as illness changed its course
will wander to the main stream
and there below the long waterfalls
and cataracts I will begin my rush
to the place I was going from the start.
I imagine looking back to see
the silted mass where a huge bend
holds sunlight in a net of evergreen
and the sky unable to bear its own
violet brilliance a moment longer.
Out of shadows where the channel
crumbles comes the raucous sound
a great blue heron makes when startled.
Scent of peppermint rides breezes
from the valley and I catch hints
of current beneath the surface
just as darkness unfurls.
There I imagine what was lost
coming together with what was gained
to pour itself at last into the sea.

Floyd Skloot
"Channel"

ACKNOWLEDGMENTS

The author wishes to acknowledge the tremendous debt he owes those who made this book possible:

To the clients/patients of NCADD/Phoenix, Desert Vista Hospital of Mesa, Arizona, Charter Behavioral Health System of Arizona and the Franciscan Renewal Center of Paradise Valley for teaching me what I truly know about therapy. To those who reviewed the manuscript and offered many valuable suggestions (Gerald S. Mayer, Ph.D.; Clay Dix; Guy Webster; Lynda Fisher; Marilyn Farley; Thomas C. Larson; Mauro Pando; Patricia A. Kenny; Anne Stephenson and, certainly, to Thomas M. Blaschko of Idyll Arbor, Inc.). To those who provided information along the way (Brian Bigelow; Bob Cox; Maggie Scott Irwin; Don Prohosky and Michael Tansy, Ph.D.). To Jayne Goldstein and Barbara Poe of the Rio Salado Chemical Dependency Program. To my valued friends Chuck New, Tommy DellaRocca, Herlinda Valles, Alfie Lavaldo and Tony Trejo. To the late Steven Glen Anderson of the East Valley Catholic Social Service for his courage and compassion despite pain and infirmity. To my parents, Wilette Lucas and the late Woody Lucas. And finally, to my longtime wife, pal and helpmate, Patricia A. Kenny for simply being her special self. All the successes of this book belong to them; all opinions and/or inaccuracies belong to me.

Contents

MEPHISTO:

When it comes to this discipline,
The way is hard to find, wrong roads abound,
And lots of hidden poison lies around
Which one can scarcely tell from medicine.

Goethe's *Faust* Pt. 1

Introduction

This book is a gift, to you, of my personal experience with the strange world of alcoholism. It is for you, the worried family member who in trying to help your problem drinker might be doing exactly the wrong thing. It is for you, the parent, spouse or lover of a problem drinker who is not sleeping through the night; who is obsessively thinking about him (Is he driving drunk? Does she have the kids in the car? I just heard a siren — is that him?); who is suffering tension headaches; or who is providing or withholding something (physical affection, creature comforts) in yet another vain attempt to make him stop killing himself. Finally, it is for you, the person who has taken such good care of an alcoholic (and everyone else!) that you are in danger of losing your self and your sanity.

In the past, you had to search high and low for a book on alcoholism; now you stumble over them as you enter a bookstore. Books are written about alcoholics by non-alcoholics who believe they know them; books are written by alcoholics who want you to "feel their pain;" books are written about what it feels like to get into treatment or to spotlight yet another vitamin, dietary or religious "breakthrough" that is untested, trivializes the problem or offers no real solution.

During my seven years as administrator and counselor with the National Council on Alcoholism and Drug Dependence (*NCADD*) affiliate in Phoenix, Arizona, I noticed myself endlessly repeating the same information to almost all my clients, their families and friends. That's not to say that all of it originated with me or that I gave each client identical advice (a practice neither therapeutic nor ethical). It's just that a vast majority of clients entered my office unaware that alcoholism (1) has nothing to do with morals or willpower; (2) is not a metaphor for social decay or anything else; (3) won't go away if you simply treat its symptoms; (4) differs greatly from social drinking; (5) is a disease of denial; (6) has nothing to do with logic; (7) lacks an easily-identified cause; (8) most often depends on concerned persons who unwittingly help sustain it; and (9) is not solved by simply putting the "plug in the jug."

The path toward understanding alcoholism (at least in this book) leads this way:

An alcoholic is a person with a pathological problem who, once he chooses to start, finds it extremely difficult to stop drinking. This clinical definition is not meant to be construed to say that an alcoholic *never* stops drinking. That notion is patently false. *Of course* alcoholics stop drinking. They may start in Albuquerque and stop in Boston. They may stop when the bar closes or when the liquor is all gone. They may, to preserve domestic tranquillity, force themselves to stop — for a while. Or, as with the hard-drinking character Brick in the Tennessee Williams play *Cat On A Hot Tin Roof*, he hears a "click" that tells him to stop. But the definition correctly infers that true alcoholics find it almost impossibly hard to put down the booze after the first drink enters the brain.

Perhaps a more helpful definition goes like this: *Alcoholism is pathological drinking which causes harm.* The harm is to the person who is drinking, to his or her enablers or to innocent bystanders — especially if cars or firearms are added to the mix. The harm may be physical or emotional — probably both. This less-clinical definition is important because, unlike the one in the above paragraph, it doesn't distinguish between alcohol abusers (who seem to be able to drink moderately if they want to) and true alcoholics (who can't). This book is for anyone who is being harmed by someone else's drinking.

Alcoholism is called a disease because it parallels what is known about other diseases such as AIDS, diabetes and cancer. Alcoholism is a *primary* disease; it's not caused by problems — it *causes* problems. And it won't go away if you merely treat its symptoms. Alcoholism is also a *chronic* disease and as with any chronic disease you must take action every single day to keep it under control.

Because of the strange nature of this deadly disease, if you have it, most often you refuse to believe it. It's called *denial*. And even if you come out of denial, you may slip back into it unless a methodical, habitual recovery program is followed. There's no logic or easily-understood cause associated with this disease; if you have it you'll never figure out why. There's no way to treat alcoholism by using another mood-altering chemical. Most alcoholics rely on the unwitting co-conspiracy of at least one other person and recovery starts when others stop "enabling" the problem drinker and get into their own recovery. There is a way to bring recovery to people who don't want help — it starts by figuring out their enabling systems and collapsing them. And if alcoholics begin recovery, there are unmistakable ways to determine if they're staying in it.

The first part of this book features an all-purpose chapter entitled *Excuses, Excuses*. Included will be every excuse you're likely to hear from your problem drinker as to why she can't seem to stop drinking and enter recovery, along with suggestions on how to neutralize each one. Later chapters will express my feelings about the issues you should be acquainted with if you're disturbed about the way your loved one drinks.

The final section, *FAQ*, answers "frequently asked questions" that parents and spouses ask regarding alcoholism.

Now, permit me to make a few observations:

- Alcoholism is a disease, one that affects your problem drinker and you. He didn't ask to have the disease but, just the same, he must take responsibility for it. No one can make him recover but him. Likewise, you didn't ask to "have" an alcoholic but, just the same, it appears that you do. And no one can take care of you but you.

- I will assume that your loved one's drinking problem is not just a minor annoyance but a problem big enough to motivate you to search for and buy a book on alcoholism. I will further assume that the drinking of your alcoholic *could* ultimately put her in jail, a divorce court, a mental institution or kill her. I suggest that you assume the same.

- I will make a case for abstinence (refraining totally from drinking alcohol) for your alcoholic. Moderation is for those who can successfully drink — we call those people social drinkers and they make up most of the adult population. If you never get into trouble with alcohol and it never interferes with your life, you probably number among them.

- The word "recovery" will mean not only abstinence but also changing attitudes to ensure that the problem drinking of your loved one doesn't return.

- There won't be much self-disclosure as this will be from the head not the heart. Suffice it to say that the author is an alcoholic who took his last drink in June of 1982, entered treatment (following a formal intervention) and very much believes in abstinence for alcoholics.

- I won't bother with statistics about recovery successes. In fact, any support group, treatment facility or hypnosis joint that tries to bend your ear about its fantastic success rate is dreaming at best and downright unethical at worst.

- Quantum physicists working in an atom's interior can pretty well predict what a trillion atomic particles will do; but they will remain uncertain of both the position and momentum of one *specific* particle. Likewise, I can predict with a fair degree of accuracy the behavior of a hundred problem drinkers; I can't predict with any degree of certainty, however, the course of one *specific* drinker — the one you love.

- I will use the convenient term "loved one" often. This may be a parent, spouse, future spouse, a lover, a companion, a concerned employer, co-worker or even a bureaucrat who knows an alcoholic who is drinking up his public assistance checks and wants him to stop.

- The reader will notice that the book often switches between "he" and "she." This is done to avoid gender bias. Alcoholism is an equal opportunity destroyer. However, I do want to note here that a woman enabling an alcoholic male is the more probable scenario. My clinical impression is that women are more compassionate in this regard and are more likely to support an alcoholic through his illness — even if that means lots of enabling. Men, for the most part, tend to de-emphasize the compassion in favor of "laying down the law."

- I won't waste time helping you figure out how often and how much your loved one drinks. To do so is to fall into the trap of negotiating with her. This book will emphasize what alcohol is doing to her life.

- I will confine myself to the subject of alcohol and alcoholism. That's not to say that the information doesn't apply to other drugs such as heroin, crack cocaine or crystal methamphetamine. It certainly *does* apply. I choose to focus on the subject of alcoholism because I am on much firmer ground discussing the disease aspect with alcoholism than with addiction to other drugs. Why? Because I believe an essential factor of alcoholism is its *insidiousness*. That is to say that alcohol (which is not considered an intense euphoriant) takes hold of people so slowly that they hardly notice they're hooked. Many consume alcohol from time to time but only around one in 10 adult Americans becomes alcoholic. Heroin, however, produces a euphoria so good that half of those who use it 10 times get hooked. The smokable form of cocaine (crack), whose users have often told me that to get another rock of crack they'd sell their grandmother to the devil, is such a powerful euphoriant that $30 worth of it could turn their sweet little old blue-haired, Bible-toting grandmother into a junkie who, for another hit, would sell *their* raggedy soul in a hot minute. Is that an illness or a disease? I'm not so sure.

- This book discusses at length the behaviors of the true alcoholic, but much of it also applies to the problem drinker who is not an alcoholic. A problem drinker is someone who drinks enough alcohol to cause harm and get into trouble but can, as a rule, stop after taking the first drink. This type of drinker will use many of the same excuses as the true alcoholic. He's destroying his life and yours. And he needs to stop. Perhaps he is one of those who will ultimately become a social drinker. It is safer to assume he will not.

- I will take no stand on whether a non-alcoholic should or should not drink alcohol. That's beyond the scope of this book.

- Finally, nothing that I present to you should be construed as a substitute for medical detoxification, primary treatment, professional counseling, psychotherapy or membership in a support group. You cannot simply read this book and sober someone up. The proper course of action upon finishing this book is to call the National Council on Alcoholism and Drug Dependence (NCADD) for a list of local counselors and resources (212-206-6770) and/or consult your local White Pages for the phone number of Al-Anon Family Groups.

Chapter 1

Excuses, Excuses

You picked up this book because something has gone wrong with your life. You've seen your loved one drink at least one too many drinks and tell you at least one too many stories. You're not sure just what the problem is or, maybe, just *who* has the problem. That's what an alcoholic does — she tells herself and those around her that her drinking is not a problem. But if it becomes a problem, she will blame you for it while becoming dependent on you to help her continue. Does that really make sense? No. But neither does the drinking.

Every day during my seven years with NCADD/Phoenix a person like you came in who was stuffed so full of stories by her alcoholic that her head was spinning. After affirming that her confusion was real and not imagined, I would often observe her almost weep with gratitude that someone finally believed her. I'd then reassure her that alcoholics don't always enjoy telling stories. Nor do they always lie on purpose. Alcoholics are often quite sincere about what they say. Let us charitably refer to such stories as promises, impaired thinking, forms of prayer, cries for help. Alcoholics have a disease that makes them lie and they've had lots of time to practice their patter. This is a big part of the disease and every alcoholic does it. It's his attempt to keep running the show. If he can get you to believe that you (or his boss or his parents or his job or his ...) are the real problem, he gets to keep drinking. If he can manage to slowly replace your world of reality with his world of delusional thinking, he wins the game. If he can get you to doubt your sanity, maybe you'll get off his back.

But you've heard one story too many. In fact, your "phony story" detector is ringing as often as your telephone.

In this chapter, I'll give you the most popular and creative stories that alcoholics use to make you believe they can't get sober and stay sober. See if you have heard them before. See if the suggestions I propose make sense. If they do, then keep reading. This book will level the playing field between you and your alcoholic.

I'm not suggesting at all that you debate your alcoholic (you'll see in Chapter 4, *Don't Look for Logic*, that appeals to logic won't work). But it doesn't mean that you must fall for this stuff either.

Let's start with the granddaddy of them all:

I'm not hurting anyone else.
Of course he's hurting someone else. Would you be reading this book if you weren't hurting? Alcoholics hurt those they love by shortening their own life span and decreasing their quality of life. They hurt their family because of inattention and lost earning potential; they steal from their employers through wasted time and lowered productivity; and by drinking and driving they pose potential harm to children or anyone else who gets in front of their car.

I promise to quit.

When all else fails, when your alcoholic is scared, it's time to start making promises. About what? Oh, about anything. Watch him reach way down into that grab bag of his and dredge up the hoary one that goes, "I'll-never-touch-another-drop-so-help-me. Just give me money (another apartment, another month in the house) — pick one — and you won't find me near another bottle of booze. That's it, that's final, end of story, case closed."

Or is it? Based on his record of repeated failures in this regard, it's always surprising to see how many family members, employers, etc. continue to fall for this. Suggestion: Tell your alcoholic, "I love you and believe you truly want to quit. But I can't believe your promises anymore. I don't want to hear you talk about what you *plan* to do. I want to *watch* you get into action and into recovery. Go get help, let me see you sober and happy for a year and we'll talk."

It's your fault.

Breathes there a spouse, parent or lover of an alcoholic who hasn't begun a counseling session with the words: "I know she's got the problem but she blames me for it?" Sad to say, but that's a very common defense mechanism. The alcoholic, rather than face discomfort about drinking her life away, is going to look around for someone to blame and *voila* — it's going to be you. "You don't do enough for me." "You've never really supported what I've done." "You haven't given me as much as so-and-so." "If you'd just get off my back." "You don't understand me." Sound familiar?

Alcoholics are going to do this as certain as the leaves fall in the autumn. Suggestion: There's nothing you can do to prevent this from happening but you can anticipate it and connect with some buddies in your own support group such as Al-Anon. You'll find it easier to tolerate if you realize that almost all alcoholics do this to their families.

You're always on my back.

This is a variation of the above-mentioned *It's your fault.* The way this game is played is for the alcoholic to deliberately pick a fight with you, race off aggrieved and convinced that no one has ever given him a break, drink all night, slink back into the house and play the same game the next day. Alcoholics become quite good at this game and many play it until they're dead. Suggestion: Most games take two to play; if you don't choose to play, there is no game. This probably won't have any effect on his decision to drink but you'll be playing with *his* head instead of him playing with *yours.*

I can stop by myself.

Another standard line. The fact is, no alcoholic seeks treatment or shows up at a support group without first trying to stop by herself. The average alcoholic does this literally dozens of times prior to seeking help or support. Suggestion: When your alcoholic says this again, think to yourself, "Why will she be able to do something today that she hasn't been able to do for the last 10 or 20 years?"

All my friends drink this way.

This excuse is so old that it already has a name — "Normalizing." Alcoholics normalize their behavior when they pretend it's nothing out of the ordinary. Suggestion: Ask yourself how many people you know have to hide alcohol around the house, sneak drinks or start each day with a beer breakfast?

I just might kill myself.

Threats of suicide should always be taken seriously. Those in the throes of the disease of alcoholism often see no way out except death by their own hand. This paragraph, however, is not about that type of suicide. It's about the person who conveniently threatens to kill himself whenever he's demanding something from you. "If you don't let me in (buy me a car) (give me money) I'll kill myself." This is not a cry for help, this is extortion. Suggestion: Tell him you love him but you will no longer enable him. (For more on this see Chapter 6 on *Enabling*.) Then call Al-Anon, go to a meeting and get the emotional support you need!

You must do such-and-such or I can't get sober.

You must get me another car, let me move back home, etc. or I can't help myself. This is putting conditions on her sobering up and you'll get the blame if she doesn't. Suggestion: Tell your alcoholic you love her and give her the phone number of a counseling service, support group meeting or NCADD affiliate. Don't allow her to put conditions on her recovery.

I'll just taper off.

Sounds easy, doesn't it? Six beers today, five tomorrow, four the day after that and so on. One big problem: If he finds it extremely difficult to stop drinking after he chooses to take the first drink, he won't be able to taper off for any extended period of time.

I don't drink for the alcohol — I'm just thirsty.

An oft-heard excuse in which the alcoholic wants you to believe that beer is to be equated with beverages such as iced tea or sodas. Suggestion: Try offering him iced tea instead of beer and see what he does. Remind yourself that even thirsty people don't polish off a case of sports drink every day.

But I'm not as bad as he is.

Alcoholics under stress can be forgiven for using the "comparative" method of diverting attention from themselves. After all, they didn't make it up, it's done all the time — often by the swellest of people. All that's needed is a person further down the road to alcoholic oblivion. It might be a neighbor, a co-worker, a celebrity or the president of Russia. By standing next to these people, your alcoholic wants to look good by comparison. Suggestion: Think to yourself, "She never compares herself to social drinkers." Ask yourself, "Just how bad does she think she must get?"

But I never get drunk.

For your alcoholic to get drunk, he must first be sober. A person who displays such tolerance that he seems to have a beer can (or a Scotch and water) in his hand whenever he's awake exists in a nether world of intoxication. Suggestion: Ask yourself the truly appropriate question, "Is he ever *sober*?"

I was standing at the supermarket liquor counter yesterday and I never once had an urge to drink.

Those with a pathological inability to handle alcohol find it extremely difficult to stop drinking once they start. Their craving, however, won't start with merely looking at bottles; it begins when they drink them. Almost any alcoholic could stand next to liquor all day if she had to. The trouble comes when she ingests it. Suggestion: Ask yourself, "Has she ever gotten drunk by simply standing next to a bottle?" Remind yourself, "It's not the 10th drink that does the damage, it's the *first* one."

But I only drink four beers every two hours and then only every other day.

As mentioned in the *Introduction,* your alcoholic probably believes that alcoholism is a numbers game. Use X-amount and he's a drunk; cut back to Y-amount and he's home free. That's why he's determined to play the game with you (and with his therapist) that goes: "I'll say how much I drink and how often, and if you think I'm alcoholic, I'll start negotiating with you." A therapist of any worth will not play this game — and you shouldn't either. It's not a matter of how much and how often. The question is "What's it doing to his life?"

If I can just get my job back, I'll be fine.
There is a feminine counterpart to this claim. It goes,
If I can just get my children back, I'll be fine.
Men, over the last few thousand years, have evidently gotten it into their heads that no problem is so important that they can't go to work and ignore it. A job is not a recovery program. Neither is motherhood. Suggestion: Remind yourself that he's always tried this. And hasn't his "workaholism" always left him exhausted and searching for something to relieve his loneliness and stress? And didn't it have the word "alcohol" written all over it?

I deserve it.
One of ways your alcoholic probably justifies her drinking is to rationalize that she deserves to be rewarded. It goes something like this: "I work my fingers to the bone all day putting food on the table for a bunch of people who don't appreciate it and if I want to drink a little when I get home who cares?" There's absolutely no doubt that all of us who work hard need compensation for our labors. But rewards are intended to be fun or relaxing. They're not meant to harm our health or interfere with our lives. Suggestion: Notice that she never says, "I work hard so I ought to be able to drink all the orange juice I can handle." The "I deserve it" syndrome is just a cover-up for problem drinking.

Well, I wasn't exactly stopped for drinking and driving.
Yes, technically he was stopped by the police because his taillight was out or he made an illegal left turn. But he was impaired. His booking slip showed a blood alcohol content of .170 and that's beyond amateur status. It's amazing how many alcoholics try to mitigate their DUI with this excuse.

True recovery will begin when he takes responsibility for putting his life and other lives in danger.

I guess I need to do a little more research.

"Doing more research" is AA slang for relapsing. Suggestion: If your loved one says, flippantly or otherwise, that she needs more research, explain to her that, "Hey, the research results are in and have been in for many years." Each time a hurting person walks into an AA meeting, she's saying that drinking doesn't work for those constitutionally incapable of stopping.

I've never been fired from work.

Variation:

I've never gotten a DUI.

This is one of the more perverse excuses as it suggests that something bad must happen for a person to be alcoholic. It's as if your child told you, "It must be safe to play on the roof because I haven't fallen off." What would you say to a friend who says, "I can't have cancer because I have perfect attendance at work?" Sorry, cancer doesn't work that way; neither does alcoholism. There are thousands of alcoholics who manage to spend their entire drinking careers without getting a DUI or missing work. Suggestion: Ask yourself just how many DUIs will it take to get this guy out of denial?

You've got to be rich to get treatment.

If you have a drinking problem and don't want to stop, wouldn't it make sense to latch on to any erroneous piece of information and use it to remain in harm's way? This is done by alcoholics who accidentally discover that some treatment centers cost a lot of money. So, all of a sudden this comes to mean *all* treatment centers cost a lot of money. Thus the argument becomes, "Yeah, I could get help if I only had $26,000." Suggestion: Keep in mind that nothing could be further from the truth. Yes, there are expensive programs which feature an extended family component; but there are also many programs affiliated with cities, churches, the United Way or the Salvation Army. NCADD affiliates around the nation often have counseling and outpatient programs based on a client's ability to pay ("sliding scale"). So-called bed scholarships for those who can document their poverty are available at many treatment centers and, of course, all Twelve-Step groups are free. Money is never an obstacle when your alcoholic desires to lead a sober life.

I need it to sleep.

An alcoholic who drinks to sleep, combat loneliness or un-wind from a stressful day often notices that, paradoxically, the alcohol she drinks soon starts giving her exactly the thing she tried to avoid. If she used it to sleep, alcohol will start keeping her awake. If she used it for stress, it'll make her tense. If she used it to get high or happy, it'll make her low and miserable. If she used it as an antidote for loneli-ness, it'll make her lonely. Suggestion: Ask yourself, "Does it seem to be working?" Or does the alcohol keep her even more awake (stressed, depressed, lonely)?

I'll have to stop having fun.

A vast majority of those who enter treatment for alcoholism do so with the black cloud of demoralization hanging over their heads. Then they'll say, "Yes, but if I stop drinking what'll I do for fun?" Suggestion: Ask yourself, "What is he doing for fun now? From the looks of him, I'd say he hasn't had fun for a long time." Which is probably true. The person who seeks treatment for alcoholism is not having fun and as a matter of fact hasn't had fun for many months or years.

I'll quit for a little while.

Anyone who says this obviously doesn't understand that true alcoholics are constitutionally incapable of stopping af-ter one drink. You may have noticed that she often stays stopped for a while. But when she drinks again, she's off and running. And then you notice that she's worse than ever. Stopping for a while won't solve her problem; maintaining abstinence a day at a time in a methodical recovery program will.

OK, I'll stop forever.

A noble idea but let's take a close look at it. There is a difference between being "dry" and being in recovery. Being "dry" means that he's simply not drinking. All too often, that translates to "he's not drinking but sure wishes he were." This does not lead to happiness, contentment or close relationships. Agreed, your alcoholic probably won't be hauled out of his car by a cop when he's dry, but the clock will tick away his life one miserable second at a time. This is not recovery. Recovery is taking responsibility for a disease he didn't ask for through a methodical, habitual program of abstinence and personal growth.

Just another $1,000 and I'll be fine.

It's not uncommon for an alcoholic to view money as a solvent to wash away all her problems. Alcoholics are often convinced that one more money fix will somehow remove their pathological problem which makes it almost impossible for them to stop drinking. It won't. Suggestion: Count how many times your alcoholic says the words "win the lottery" in a single 24-hour period.

My drinking is just a bad habit which I can easily break.

A habit is what Nature uses to free us from thinking about things while doing them. Thus a driver will travel miles down the road without being conscious of drinking coffee and shifting gears. The word habit does not describe alcoholism. Spending all his waking hours securing his supply, drinking and then being hung over is a malady which depends upon your loved one making one conscious choice after another.

I'll get sober just as soon as I get back on my feet.

This belongs to the Cart-Before-the-Horse school of addiction management. You hear it often. Translated, it means "My recovery is still a very low priority and I've got places to go and people to meet." Suggestion: You may wish to remind yourself that he's had ample opportunity over the last few months or years to get back on his feet and he's always failed. That next job or that next relationship is not a recovery program for alcoholism.

When I stop drinking, I never have withdrawal.

What your alcoholic is probably referring to are the classic signs of withdrawal: seizures, shakes and hallucinations. Suggestion: Ask yourself if your alcoholic is failing to mention how often she displays much less dramatic withdrawal symptoms: nervousness, irritability, anger at not being able to drink for a while or anxiety as to whether enough cases of beer, wine or distilled spirits are on hand.

I'm too old to quit.

Variation:

I'm too young to quit.

Obviously those who say the former are so-called senior citizens which means they're always the author's age plus 10 years. Suggestion: Ask yourself, "Is anyone ever too old (or too young) to come to each day with joy?"

Let me stay with you until I get it together.

When will that be? Tomorrow? Next month? Never? Always being available to rescue an alcoholic who's in trouble again is enabling. It reinforces his notion that if he makes a mess, you'll be there to clean it up. Is it any wonder that he'll continue to drink as long as you provide a safety net worthy of the Barnum & Bailey Circus?

I promise I'll never hit you or the kids again.
Promises. Promises. Hitting people is a violent act and hitting those you live with is called domestic violence. And bear in mind that the term "hitting" includes any pushing or shoving. Domestic violence so often occurs when a person has been drinking that it seems to be little more than just another symptom of alcoholism. As in "when my husband stops drinking, I know that he'll stop hitting me." Not so. The tendency toward violence must be considered as a stand-alone problem — that means it exists with or without a drinking problem. Many alcoholics drink without ever becoming violent and many violent persons don't have a drinking problem. Many alcoholics become dry but the violence continues. Don't wait for him to stop drinking before you get help. You may be dead by that time (if that time ever comes!). Don't wait for the name calling to escalate into shoving and then into hitting and beating. Don't simply react to him. You must act now. Call your local United Way or a nearby women's shelter (they're in the Yellow Pages under *Social Service Organizations*) and get advice on how to safely remove yourself from the home. I offer the same advice to men who are victims of domestic violence. Get yourself and your children someplace safe.

Domestic violence is much more than tearful promises — it's matter of life and death.

I was only kissing (touching) her because I was drunk.
How convenient. By the time alcoholics get very far into their disease, they catch on that there's nothing they can't blame on their drinking. "I forgot to pay the bills/feed the dog/renew my drivers license because I started drinking." And this is the same guy who can tell you the score of each Chicago Bears/Green Bay Packers game from 1941 on! So

don't be surprised if he decides to claim sexual abuse or sexual infidelity is the result of too much liquor. As we discussed above, domestic violence is not a symptom of alcoholism. Neither is sexual abuse or sexual infidelity. Your proper response is to separate that issue from his alcoholism and take care of your needs or your children's needs. Make a call to a counseling office (they're in the Yellow Pages under *Social Service Organizations*) and let them support you in the difficult choices that you soon must make.

I can't be an alcoholic; I don't live on skid row.
This is a variation of the ever-popular:
I can't be an alcoholic because I don't have cirrhosis of the liver.
In the last few decades, it has caught the public fancy that all alcoholics either live in seedy parts of town or have terminal liver problems — or both. The persistence of this notion is astonishing. When lecturing on alcoholism, I often ask what percentage of alcoholics would meet these qualifications? "Most of them" is the usual answer. Suggestion: Arm yourself with carefully researched statistics which show that only 3-5% of all alcoholics reside on the "other side of the tracks" and only a like amount have cirrhosis of the liver. Cirrhosis is an insidious disease and there are plenty of ways for your alcoholic to die prior to getting it. There's suicide, homicide, car wrecks, domestic accidents, work accidents and death by exposure to heat or cold — to name but a few.

I don't like support groups.
Of course your alcoholic doesn't like support groups. She denies that she has a problem and those in support groups spend their time talking about the very problem that she denies having. If she listens to them too long, she might start identifying with them and then she must do something about her drinking.

Your alcoholic may be sent to AA (a little nudge from the judge) as part of a jail diversion program. Odds are high that he'll sit on the back row, stare at his shoes and drink coffee. Failing to identify with other alcoholics, he'll say, "I don't like those meetings." Or "I don't want to spill my guts in front of other people."

Those who don't believe they have a drinking problem will usually not like counseling, treatment or AA. Send a person who doesn't believe in God to church and they won't like that either. Having some idea of powerlessness over alcohol and a desire to stop having pain in his life is his ticket to success in a support group. If he goes with the idea that the group can help him, he'll be surprised how much he'll get out of it.

Listening to the stories of others makes me depressed.

No one knows why this happens, but I've heard it too many times to discount it. I have a hunch that many alcoholics are somewhat narcissistic and haven't learned to empathize or "feel the pain" of others. Thus, when confronted with such pain in a support group, their only option is to re-feel their own pain which makes them uncomfortable to the point that they shun meetings and drink again. Or perhaps certain AA stories cause long-repressed guilt to surface which she hasn't yet learned how to handle without alcohol. Suggestion: Be mindful that the personal stories told by AA members center around "what it was like" (insanity and pain), "what happened" (awareness and enlightenment), and "what it's like now" (freedom and joy). As she hears each story, she may be focusing solely on the pain of "what it was like." She should be encouraged to keep attending, to de-focus from the "problem" part of each story and learn to listen for the speaker's "solution."

I went to one support group meeting and didn't go back.
Most people who attend their first support group (be it AA
or Al-Anon) feel somewhat apprehensive until they learn to
speak the language of recovery and begin meeting people
who have similar problems. Most towns or cities of any size
have many meetings per week. If your alcoholic desires to
stay sober, he should sample as many meetings as he can
and make a habit of attending the ones he's comfortable
with. Suggestion: Remind yourself that he probably didn't
like the first bar he went to either. Did he stop drinking? No,
he just went around to different bars and found a few he fell
in love with!

I just can't identify with other alcoholics.
Isolation is to alcoholism what fertilizer is to flowers; it
causes them to grow. So, it wouldn't be surprising if your
alcoholic has a tendency to shun people, places, things and
situations. If so, her life may come down to a bar, a kitchen
table, a TV and a bottle — her own personal skid row, as it
were. She may (as newcomers often do) carry that isolation
right into Alcoholics Anonymous. She'll look around and
compare herself with others. "I'm not as bad as that drunk;
this or that person is too highly educated; I spilled more alcohol than that woman ever drank; I never got DUIs," and
so on. Alcoholics, the old joke goes, are like nudists; they
never make progress until they stop *comparing* and start *identifying* — until they start tearing down their walls. When
your alcoholic learns to identify with another alcoholic (an
old person, a high-schooler, a member of a biker club, an
ethnic minority or a member of the opposite gender) as a
fellow sufferer who sought relief from pain by drinking alcohol — how it worked for a while and then stopped working forever — she's on her way to true recovery.

AA meetings are too smoky.

That's the way it used to be. Until somewhat recently, AA members joked that they could find a meeting blindfolded. All they had to do was walk until they smelled coffee, cigarette smoke and heard laughter. Once in a while one stumbled upon a no-smoking meeting but they were rare. With the 1990s, however, that all changed. The tidal wave of healthy lifestyles and smoke-free environments swept over such venerable smoke-filled establishments as AA. Today, it's rare to find a meeting where one *can* smoke. Cigarette smoke is no longer a barrier to those who wish to stop drinking.

I like AA but I don't like all that God stuff.

A common reaction. AA is not religious, however it is very *spiritual*. As a newcomer, your alcoholic may attend an AA meeting, hear the word "God" and make an incorrect assumption that it's some sort of religion. Religions usually have three things in common: They are formally organized, each denomination tends to believe the same way and each tends to be *exclusive*. Religious dogma does not exist in AA. Your alcoholic may come to believe in a Higher Power according to how he individually chooses to believe. Most members refer to their Higher Power as God, Jesus, Yahweh, Lord Buddha, the Four Winds, the Pollen Path, Allah, Krishna, a Divine Creator or the Circle of Life — among many others. Noted psychiatrist R. D. Laing even said that God could be referred to as the Not-Self! Recovering people may regard, as a Power Greater than themselves, any serious group of recovering alcoholics. It doesn't matter. AA wants to be *inclusive*. In theory, a meeting could consist of Catholics, Protestants, Jews, Navajos, Buddhists, Mormons, Shintoists, Universalists, Christian Scientists, Quakers and Hindus all keeping their own rich traditions while together they celebrate sobriety as a gift from One who is more powerful than they are.

AA is designed to be no one's ticket to Heaven. In fact, the concept of an afterlife is among the many outside issues about which AA traditionally has no opinion. Suggestion: One is safe in defining "spiritual" as "that which is not material." Think to yourself whether your alcoholic hasn't had ample time to prove that material items such as other people, lovers, lucrative jobs, cars, fine houses, money and property could get him sober. If they haven't, then AA says it may be time for him to abandon a dependency on material things in favor of spirituality. AA's approach to spirituality won't save his soul but it will help save his life.

Chapter 2

It's a Disease

*Therapists understand that each alcoholic wants to
be offered an "alcohol patch" or a tap from a magic
wand with the words, "Arise and go, your disease
has been removed."*

If you've paid any attention at all to the news media during
the last few years, I suspect you've come to the conclusion
that alcoholism results from unresolved inner conflicts,
stress and pain avoidance, sensation-seeking, dysfunctional
families, aberrant brain chemicals, lack of willpower and a
wrathful God. All of these theories are the products of
someone's imagination; none are proven, none are likely to
be proven and none have anything to do with your desire to
get a loved one into recovery.

My definition of alcoholism assigns no blame, has nothing to do with white rats in a maze, easily fits into a therapist's office, seeks not a cause and lacks the whiff of acade-

27

mia. There are no three-dollar words, no psycho-babble and no lengthy questionnaires entitled, "So you think you're an alcoholic!"

Clearly and simply, *an alcoholic is a person with a pathological problem who, once he chooses to start, finds it extremely difficult to stop drinking* — an explanation so solid as to satisfy even the definition-obsessed Socrates. And as was stated in the *Introduction*, a perhaps more valuable definition for you, the reader, is, *alcoholism is pathological drinking which causes harm.* Keep in mind that while you may occasionally take a drink of alcohol to be sociable, unwind or perhaps to feel more sophisticated, a true alcoholic will most often find himself unable to stop after that first drink is taken.

These clinical and less-than-clinical definitions of alcoholism are not only brief but remarkable for what they *don't* say. They say nothing about sin or lack of character. They do not say that your alcoholic is a bad person who needs to be good; rather, that he's an ill person who needs to get well. They don't say that alcoholism is a metaphor for a doomed and Godless civilization. They don't say that alcoholism makes sense or has anything to do with logic. Notice too that they don't concern themselves with how often your alcoholic starts drinking or hint that alcoholism spontaneously improves. There's nothing in the definitions about how much your alcoholic earns, his skin color, level of education, socio-economic status, political party or whether she's a close personal friend of Oprah. They clearly say that (1) while he may not start often (periodic drinkers might not start but once or twice a year), a true alcoholic will most often be unable to stop drinking once alcohol goes down the hatch; and (2) it won't be long before an alcohol *abuser* starts causing physical and emotion harm to himself and to those around him.

What the definitions do say, through their use of the word *pathological*, is that alcoholism seems to be a disease, one with symptoms and an easily-predicted course of action.

How good are these definitions? So flexible that readers who aren't addicted to a mood-altering chemical may go back to the two previously-mentioned definitions, drop the word "drinking," insert the mood alterer of their choice — food, TV, gambling, relationships, sex, work, Internet chat rooms, exercise, shopping, wealth or power — and discover that the definitions stand as true as the flag at Ft. McHenry after heavy British bombardment.

I further believe it to be true that alcoholics (whether they're aware of it or not) understand these definitions as you understand your child. As a non-addicted person, however, you might accept the definitions and make them work for you, but there's a good chance you'll *never* understand them.

It's terminal and predictable

If a person is alcoholic and doesn't treat it (put it into remission through a methodical program of recovery), the disease of alcoholism will terminate in two classic ways: entry into an institution (mental hospital or jail) or, ultimately, death. Don't believe me? Read the papers and watch TV. Every day, they'll discuss a well-known person who acts out his problem drinking in public. The news anchor will say that the celebrity has disappeared to some hospital for "exhaustion," is in jail on some alcohol-related charge or has been picked up by an expensive Beverly Hills mortuary, kept cold for a few days and then packed off to some bucolic cemetery.

Closer to home, think about what happened to Aunt Wanda, Uncle Ralph or even Cousin Carl. Or that co-worker you know who on week-ends keeps her hand wrapped around a cold one from morning to night. Where are they? I would add here that the downward progress of many alcoholics may be so slow that one may be tempted to say, "Well, my brother-in-law's a drunk but he's been one for 40 years. He's not in jail, a clinic or dead." But perhaps your brother-in-law is not telling you about the hangovers, the "whiskey bumps" on his car and the occasional DUI he's received.

The disease is also *predictable,* a Latin word made up of two smaller words: "prae" (before) and "dicere" (say). In other words, predictable means that like a pool shot, you can "call" it in advance.

Some decades ago, Dr. E. M. Jellinek clearly saw what is sure to happen to an untreated alcoholic who begins his great downward slide. Jellinek graphically translated what he saw into what is known as the Jellinek Chart, or V-Chart, so called because it resembles a giant letter V. (See the Jellinek Chart on page 171.) The left side of the V is the slippery slope down which all alcoholics must go; it's where the consequences are. The right side is the gradual, upward climb to recovery and freedom.

The left side depicts what an alcoholic will experience as she begins "hitting bottom." It begins innocently enough with small problems such as "sneaking drinks" or "feelings of guilt" and then proceeds to more painful, ever-worsening problems such as "physical deterioration," "vague spiritual desires" and "complete defeat admitted."

On the right side of the V-Chart is the upward path of recovery. The idea is to leave the left side for the right side as quickly as possible. Those who can do this have a low tolerance to pain; those who can't, and there are many, seem to have a high tolerance. At the bottom of the V-Chart is the trough (much like John Bunyan's Slough of Despond) and life there is unreal and painful. The closer she drifts to this trough (like a daredevil in a barrel who goes nearer and nearer the drop-off at Niagara Falls), the harder it is to get out. Many have the idea that they can tarry in the trough until it's time to get into recovery. But the trick is to stay alive while you're getting motivated. Some get into the trough and reach some sort of spiritual awakening while there. But often it's too late for these so-called "11:59 alcoholics" and their shattered physical condition from all those years of drinking soon takes them to the grave.

My point is this: Jellinek, after years of work with suffering alcoholics, noticed that he could plot their downward course with astonishing accuracy. Therapists far less brilliant than Jellinek can too; give them a minute and they can pretty well predict what an untreated alcoholic is in for.

It's progressive

Alcoholism is not only a terminal disease, it's also *progressive*. The term progressive means (and I've always been uncomfortable with using a word like "progressive" to indicate a downward course) that the disease of alcoholism gets worse, never better. Ask any alcoholic. Ask him if his inability to stop drinking has made his life better or worse. If he's honest, he'll say "worse."

Personally, I never saw anyone pop their head into a support group or alcoholism clinic and say, "Hey, I'm an alcoholic and I just relapsed. Everyone come out and join me because it's wonderful out here. Sex is better, relationships are better, the cops all like me and I've certainly made my banker, my spouse and the Internal Revenue Service very happy." No, it has never happened and it won't. What happens is that the relapser has another bad relationship, loses more money, is slapped with another DUI and gets further in debt to the IRS. That's not to mention the crushing guilt, remorse and suicidal thoughts that often accompany relapse.

It should be intuitively obvious that alcoholism gets worse when alcohol is consumed. But hang on to your hat: alcoholism gets worse even when alcohol is *not consumed*. This goes against intuition, but it's true. It means that even if your alcoholic stops drinking, her disease will stay active and slowly put on muscle.

Alcoholics may not know why this happens but chances are they've experienced it first-hand. Maybe they "swore off" in order to prove to themselves or a loved one that they can't possibly be alcoholic — or if they are, they could handle it themselves. They went "dry" for a week, a month, a year or a decade. Without some sort of methodical program of recovery, they return to drinking. Because they were drinking X-amount of alcohol when they stopped, they expected to return to the same amount when they resumed. As any alcoholic can tell you, they didn't. They returned to a level of consumption they would have already achieved had they not stopped drinking. Why? Because their alcoholism continued unabated during their abstinence.

Perhaps an apt metaphor for this perplexing truth can be found in Oscar Wilde's *The Picture of Dorian Gray* where a portrait of the London dandy, locked away in an attic, visibly ages and deteriorates while Gray himself keeps the outward appearance of serene beauty. The hidden portrait can be seen as the disease of alcoholism which continues to deteriorate while the person himself attends to his inner and outer self in a program of recovery.

The AA old-timers know this and that's why you see them in meetings even after 20 or 50 years of sobriety. They know that while they've been practicing their recovery, their disease has been working out at the health club!

It's incurable

The disease of alcoholism is also *incurable*; if you have it, you may overcome it but it's not going to go away. I believe this is the single most denied, misunderstood, ignored, suppressed, forgotten, disassociated and repressed notion in the entire alcohological zoo.

There are three basic types of alcoholics. First are those who will never concede that they have lost the ability to drink successfully. A second type believes he'll regain control of his alcohol when he gets his life back together. After his wife returns, after he gets yet another job, after they get their kids back from the local Child Protective Services, he'll reckon he is now cured and return to drinking. This won't work because once he chooses to take the first drink, his life will get sick again — perhaps fatally. And the third type will find no reason to "road test" his drinking again, will join a methodical program of recovery and never leave it.

Therapists understand that each alcoholic wants to be offered an "alcohol patch" or a tap from a magic wand with the words "Arise and go, your disease has been removed." But they can't. There's no such patch and no such wand.

It's treatable

On the plus side, this disease is also *treatable* and *preventable*. Treatment usually comes in the form of a methodical, results-based approach which directs an alcoholic's energies toward admitting, confronting and resolving her life-threatening situation. Treatment is where she goes from the left to the right side of the Jellinek Chart. Treatment is usually of two types: inpatient and outpatient.

Inpatient, which is getting scarcer due to the reluctance of third-party payers to reimburse it, is the most intense form of treatment as the alcoholic is expected to stay in the inpatient facility for a specific amount of time. Inpatient is sometimes called *milieu* therapy meaning it is designed to almost totally control the focus and environment of the alcoholic so that positive habits may be instilled. Milieu therapy is very structured, with every hour of the day devoted to some form of physical, emotional, psychological and spiritual improvement.

Outpatient treatment is regarded as less intensive; but let no one believe for a second that outpatient treatment lacks its share of intense moments. It's just that the client or patient doesn't sleep there; rather, she commutes to the outpatient clinic a prescribed number of times per week. Fifteen to 20 years ago, you could count on an outpatient program lasting four hours a night, every weekday night for a month. During the last few years, again partly because of a lack of managed care reimbursement, most outpatient programs have been whittled to three hours a night for three nights a week with mandatory support group meetings to get the newly-sober alcoholic through the weekends.

As might be expected, therapists must carefully assess each patient to determine their appropriateness for either an inpatient or outpatient setting. Roughly seven things are looked for:

1. Is the patient sufficiently detoxified from alcohol to dispense with medical assistance?
2. Does the patient have friends who don't use drugs or drink alcoholically?
3. Can the patient successfully live away from the treatment center and commute on a thrice-a-week basis?
4. Is the patient free from serious mental illness?
5. Does the patient have family support for his recovery?
6. If the patient has a history of outpatient treatment, was it successful? and
7. Is the patient motivated?

If any one of these questions is answered no, he might be better off going inpatient — insurance permitting. Why? Because intensive milieu therapy provides medical attention, a ready-made peer group (an *elective* family) and a temporary retreat from the pressures of everyday life.

Detoxification — or "detox" — often precedes entry into primary treatment but relatively few people have a severe enough problem — or good enough health insurance — to take advantage of it. The goal of detox is not self-discovery — that comes later. Detox provides medical help toward getting alcohol out of the system. If enough alcohol has been consumed for a long enough period of time, a medically-assisted withdrawal is a must.

Withdrawal from alcohol is a very serious matter. The classical symptoms are seizures (which are generally indistinguishable from an epileptic seizure), hallucinations and shakes (delirium tremens). The rule of thumb is that alcohol withdrawal usually takes only four to five days. That's the good news. The bad news is that withdrawal from alcohol is so short (compared to withdrawal from many other drugs) that it just may kill you if you're already too far along in your disease or not under medical supervision.

So serious is withdrawal from alcohol that most addictionists consider it far more life threatening than withdrawal from cocaine, crystal methamphetamine or even heroin. The only other family of drugs whose withdrawal is considered life-threatening is the group of sedative-hypnotics (Valium, Xanax, etc.) The *half-life* of these drugs is so long (Valium's half-life is 20-50 hours) as to make withdrawal from them a long, painful and dangerous process.

The dramatic rise of managed health care and major cutbacks in government spending have called a halt to the heady days of detox funding. So much so that many clinics are instituting "social" detox centers where alcoholics and addicts with less severe problems seek withdrawal treatment on a daily, or outpatient basis. This is being seen as a far more economical way to provide treatment; whether it is as effective remains to be seen.

It's preventable

The fact that the disease of alcoholism is also *preventable* may strike you as odd until you remember how effective education can be. For instance, a person may discover that with both parents alcoholic, it might be best to make an informed decision in favor of abstinence. Others may discover new,

more appropriate ways to cope with developmental problems. One NCADD client in the early 1990s was only 18. He
stumbled home from a teen party one night and his worried
parents brought him in for counseling. As it turned out, the
youth was shy and inexperienced around girls his age. Becoming embarrassed at a party, he began drinking to calm
his nerves and overdid it. With education about other options for overcoming shyness (dance lessons, etc.), he
learned to forego the use of alcohol which he admitted never
liking in the first place.

Prevention research often focuses on the recognition of
social and biological "markers" that may indicate future
problems with alcohol. *Social* markers include an environment of family secrets, inconsistent parenting, the absence of
communication and feeling unloved by parents. Children
raised in such an atmosphere will benefit from consistent
rules and the development of healthy communication skills.

Biological markers include childhood depression and
conduct disorders. Children demonstrating these markers
might be saved from starting down the road to alcoholism
by learning to cope with their impulsiveness and negative
feelings. As the *Frequently Asked Questions* section of this
book will later demonstrate, almost any child with social and
biological markers can learn to cope with life without re-
sorting to chemicals if they have at least one accepting, un-
conditionally-loving role model (teacher, friend, etc.).

Other methods of prevention include higher levels of
beverage alcohol taxation, tougher DUI penalties, laws that
raise the legal drinking age and laws that restrict access to
alcohol by minors.

Chapter 3

Don't Look for a Cause

Mad let us grant him then. And now remains
That we find out the cause of this effect,
Or rather say, the cause of this defect,
For this effect defective comes by cause...

Hamlet, Act II, Scene II

Correct me if I'm way off base here, but I have a hunch that as a loved one of an alcoholic, you've invested much time and energy trying to find a *cause* for his alcoholism. Perhaps you've lived with him long enough to notice the many concurrent problems he seems to have. Things like poor financial habits, poor coping skills, anger, grief and depression. And why wouldn't he have these problems? Drink alcoholically for any length of time and you'll squander your dollars, become extremely frustrated, take your anger out on loved ones and end up depressed at best and homicidal or suicidal at worst.

So you may be tempted to think that all these problems are the cause of his alcoholism. A note of caution, however. The mental and behavioral health professions have spent many decades looking for one so it's not likely you'll succeed where they've always failed.

No one really knows why but human beings seem to take comfort in the idea that every effect must have a well-understood cause. If there's a good effect, look for the cause and learn from it. If there's an evil effect, find the cause and destroy it.

Thousand-ton aircraft fly (an effect) because G. B. Venturi and the Wright Brothers noticed that a bird wing moving through the air creates a pressure differential which results in lift (a cause). Likewise, when politicians notice voters responding to public opinion polls a certain way (an effect), they make it their job to discover which policy is making them do so (the cause). Shakespeare's addled Polonius (quoted at the beginning of this chapter) wrongly thought that Hamlet's madness (an effect) stemmed from unrequited love for his doomed daughter Ophelia (a cause). The quotation succinctly captures the confusion that awaits if you continue to look for a cause for alcoholism.

Perhaps the attachment to the cause = effect equation stems from the fact that in normal life, under normal conditions, the equation works. But just as Newtonian physics fails when an object approaches the speed of light, so too does the cause = effect equation fail when one approaches the "speed of alcoholism."

If an alcoholism counselor sees a thousand alcoholics and family members a year, she will hear a thousand theories as to why the alcoholism is happening. The 8 am client will guess that she became alcoholic because life with her parents was abusive and dysfunctional. Naturally, she sought to get away from the shame of such abuse and found relief in a bottle. The 9 am client will say that his parents were such geeks, nerds and dweebs that naturally he chose alcohol as a way of rebelling against such squares. The 10 am client will then make a wonderful case for being an alcoholic because he never had parents. Each of these theories are mutually exclusive; yes, each of them can cause emotional pain; but none come close to producing a cause. Even the great Sigmund Freud, the father of psychoanalysis ("treatment of the id by the odd"), was convinced that alcoholism was caused by suppressed masturbation!

You might have noticed this in other areas of behavioral health as well. During the summer of 1997, the news media began to report that countries such as Argentina had three times the incidence of anorexia as the United States. "Devotion to fashion makes Argentine girls anorexic!" read one breathless headline. Even accounting for the tendency of headline writers to banner articles they don't read carefully, it is still very much of a stretch to think that being a slave to what writer Tom Wolfe called the "social X-ray look" could account for the poor teeth, loss of bone mass and brain cells that comes with the compulsion to starve yourself to death.

Let's assume that, miracle of miracles, you found the cause of your loved one's alcoholism. That, yes, it was inconsistent parenting, improper toilet training, stress-avoidance, sensation-seeking or sexual abuse. That, yes, it was an attempt to find meaning in a cold, unfeeling universe. That, yes, it was an attempt to shrink life and its many problems down to the size of a shot glass. What exactly do you do with that information? Loved ones hardly ever give it a thought, so obsessive is their search for a cause. Can you go back 40 years and undo mistakes made by his mom and dad? Certainly he may (and should) seek out a trained and certified therapist to help him deal with any trauma, but it won't change anything that happened and it won't cure his alcoholism. It's like trying to find the exact pothole that caused you to lose control of your car. You may find it and satisfy your curiosity about it — heck, you can even take a photo of it. But regardless of how much you scrutinize the pothole, the fact remains that you just had a car wreck and must do something about it.

The author submits that assuming a cause for alcoholism is not only naïve but dangerous. Your alcoholic might be tempted to think: "I am an alcoholic because I was sexually abused (or am depressed, etc.) and therefore alcoholism therapy must wait until I complete trauma or depression counseling." And *you* might be tempted to think, "She's that way because I wasn't a good enough mother." Or, "I don't know where I failed but she started drinking again." This could lead to painful demoralization and hinder your eventual recovery.

It may be safer to stick to what we know about alcoholism and stay out of what we don't know. We know there are a number of issues almost always *associated* with alcoholism. These may be called *symptoms* of the alcoholism or even *contributing factors*, and you don't have to scratch your alcoholic too deeply to find them. Yes, they may set your loved one up for alcoholism or make him choose to take the first drink. But they cannot be said to cause it.

The following issues are caused by alcoholism. But neither singly nor in combination can they be said to *cause* alcoholism.

Depression

Between 30-40% of all alcoholics also have mood disorders, usually depression. Further, 10-15% of alcoholics attempt suicide — no doubt a highly underreported statistic. And alcoholics are 20 times more likely to die than the "normal" population.

With one out of 20 American adults afflicted with it, you might think that depression could easily be defined. It can't. Ask a Native American living in the Arctic to define snow and chances are you'll get a lengthy list of snow types. Ask a mental health professional to define depression and you'll get a discussion of chronic, clinical and major depression; dysthymia; dysphoria; unipolar and bipolar depression; unhappiness; despondency; discontent; lethargy; gloominess; seasonal affective disorder (SAD); dejection; discouragement; *ennui;* malaise; *fiaca;* the "blahs" and the "blues."

The spectrum ranges from "normal" depression experienced by those reacting to grief to "less normal" depression (dysthymia, a milder yet persistent depression), all the way to fully abnormal and disabling (clinical) depression, the symptoms of which are severe.

The term "secondary depression" is used to mean a depressive disorder that accompanies a "primary disorder" like alcoholism. No one is ever sure which comes first, alcoholism or depression — although much of the depression accompanying alcoholism seems to be secondary. Obviously, alcohol is categorized as a type of "depressant," the consumption of which will lead to a so-called "depressogenic" lifestyle in which depression is the overriding affect (feeling).

Likewise, many alcoholics report feelings of depression *prior* to their use of alcohol. Most behavioral health professionals believe that many take up alcohol to medicate their essential depression. But one thing is sure: depression doesn't *cause* alcoholism; it's much safer to say that alcoholism can cause depression.

Thoughts of suicide

Not all alcoholics have entertained the idea of taking their lives — however, many come to believe there's no other option. Once an alcoholic begins the cycle of drinking, chances are good he will become unable to visualize life without alcohol.

It was once thought that only depression caused suicide. Evidence is starting to pile up, however, that feelings of *desperation* — an inability to visualize change — is a better predictor of suicidal risk. Both depression and desperation are states of unhappiness. Depression has to do with problems *within* the individual; desperation (or hopelessness) deals more with the individual as he relates to his world. Thus, an alcoholic may not be depressed but his cognitive worldview may lead him to the conclusion that his condition is not going to change and that suicide is his only option.

Understanding the key role that desperation plays in suicidal thoughts may finally explain one puzzling aspect of pre-suicide behavior. Devastated families left to cope with the suicide of a loved one often report that, "Just before he shot himself, he seemed creative and happy." So, how could he kill himself if he wasn't depressed? It's because he made the decision to end his life in a state of confusion and disappointment and making that decision, ironically, curtailed his depression.

It's wisdom for you to shun platitudes ("it's wrong to end your own life," or "look on the bright side of things") when talking to the suicidal person. This is more about you and your philosophy (and perhaps your own anxiety) than it is about him and he'll quickly pick up on it. It will be more therapeutic to ask what brings the person to suicide as an option — to forsake rebuke in favor of the more compassionate question, "Why do you feel so bad?"

If a suicide is accomplished, family survivors will rarely discuss it among themselves. Working with counselors, survivors will learn to address their lack of communication and the amount of guilt they are carrying. Guilt is the single most consistent feeling associated with surviving families and most of it is undeserved.

Anger

It's easy to understand how angry most alcoholics are when they come into therapy. Things are not going well in their lives; the alcohol which was once a friend has now become an enemy; the drink which was once a medicine is now a poison. Their disease has caused such a distortion of reality and lack of healthy coping/communication skills that life for them is but one frustration after another. But this anger is *appropriate*; that is, such frustration can be expected to result in anger.

However, there is a second type of anger your loved one may display — anger *without* an easily identifiable cause. A therapist will become concerned if an alcoholic says, "I have no idea why I'm angry; in fact, it's puzzled me for 40 years." That's quite another type of anger and if the therapist is a betting man, he'll line up at the ticket window marked "Early childhood."

It should not be surprising to discover that parents and children have an unspoken agreement that says, "I'll meet your needs" whereas the child expects (perhaps subconsciously) those needs to be met. The author, when growing up in the 1940s and 1950s, heard adults often say, "Yes, he's a jerk, but his kids are clean and there's always food on the table." As if that were all the parent could be expected to provide. Today, however, it is generally understood that children need much more than just clothing, school books and an occasional meal. Society is coming to understand that parents must meet the *emotional* needs of their children.

When emotional support fails to materialize, children perceive (but can't articulate) that something is missing. Often, anger develops. Of course, that anger needs to be processed but how can a child deal with anger? So, year after year, decade after decade, the anger just sits there. Then all of a sudden, the child who is now an adult finds herself angry. In fact, her friends begin to ask, "Why are you always so furious?" But you're asking the wrong person; she hasn't a clue; she's just as stymied as you are.

If she seeks non-professional help (a close friend, for instance) she might be told to "grow up." At the very least, her friend will appeal to the stoicism of adulthood by saying, "Hey, what's past is past; let it go; are you going to blame mom and dad all your life?" This appeal to logic won't work. In fact, it may just confuse her all the more. It is not just a *cognitive* problem — it's not just in the head; it's also an *affective* or "feeling" problem which can be solved by a professional therapist addressing the conflicted inner feelings first laid down in childhood.

Still a third type of anger is that used to mask fear, guilt and shame. If you're looking to wall out such feelings there's no better mortar than anger. Don't want to take an honest look at your actions? Get angry. Got something in your past you'd like to hide? Get angry. Don't want to admit you're afraid? Hate something. It wouldn't be at all surprising to discover that both you and your alcoholic tend to hide behind a wall of anger when the disease of alcoholism has you both scared to death.

Guilt and shame

Your alcoholic will undoubtedly be despondent or disappointed over things he's done — this is called *guilt*. The interesting thing about guilt is that you must actually do something (or fail to do something) in order to feel it. For instance, alcoholics violate their personal code of morals: they disappoint people they love; cheat on their spouses; make one promise after another; can be counted on to get drunk at exactly the wrong moment, and so on.

Recovery for such guilt begins when the alcoholic goes to an AA meeting, introduces himself as a member and shares his story with others. He'll soon discover that, just like him, all other members must deal with their guilt as well and he won't feel so alone. And remember, no alcoholic has ever shown up at an AA meeting having done something so heinous that members had to think up a new word to describe it!

We have seen that guilt appears when a person *does* something. *Shame*, however, is something a person *is*. Recovering alcoholics shed guilt pretty fast; shame, however, can hang on like a bad case of the flu. Children encounter shame when they continually receive the unspoken message that they must never betray to the outside world that their family is much less than it appears or that it seems to have its ancestral home on Tobacco Road. As a rule, they won't verbally betray this secret. What they will do, however, is wear the secret on their sleeves and act it out whenever anyone is watching. This will evoke from others the feelings they have towards their parents but are unable to express directly to their face. This certainly doesn't come close to an appropriate coping skill but it will get them through childhood. However, you can bet that it will give them problems when they reach adulthood (see following section on Lack of Adequate Coping Skills).

Shame is noticed by therapists when a client avoids eye contact (often with the face being literally hidden by the hands or the hair) or verbally describes close relationships they abruptly discontinued without ever knowing why.

Trying to cope with shame explains why many children of alcoholics become so-called "family heroes" and overachieve to the extent that they ultimately wear themselves out. Becoming a family hero is a child's logic: "If I can just get straight A's, always look immaculate, excel in sports, stay on the student council and the cheerleading squad and perhaps get chosen as homecoming royalty, then no one will have a clue that my family is such a complete mess."

No one has ever illustrated the shame spiral better than Antoine de Saint-Exupery in his classic children's book *The*

Little Prince. On one planet, the little prince encounters the Tippler (chapter IX) who drinks to mitigate the shame of drinking!

Stress

Alcoholics (especially men) seem to take pride in their perception that the stress of their jobs magically turns them into drunks. Carpenters grin and wink when they tell you that those who fashion wood into functional objects are surely the world's heaviest drinkers. Auto mechanics, teamsters, policemen, firemen, dock workers, maintenance men, farmers and cowboys will tell you the same.

This is not just a blue-collar phenomenon. Many's the journalist who has told me, "Well, you know the way it is with us H. L. Mencken, Westbrook Pegler, James Agee, Ernest Hemingway-types. I'd say we scribes might just be the real heavyweights of the drinking world."

Once I responded with a letter to the editor of the *Arizona Republic* regarding a feature article which intimated that the high rate of alcoholism among fire fighters and police officers (18% and 25%, respectively) was due to stress. While affirming that those important occupations certainly garner more than their fair share of stress, I suggested that such stress had nothing to do with causing the alcoholism. Indeed, the article seemed to come to the distressing conclusion that because of such stress, those public servants could be *forgiven* for drinking so much. I suggested they become familiar with NCADD statistics which showed their high rates of alcoholism still fell below those of news reporters and editors (20%); carpenters, (25%); aircraft-engine mechanics (26%); vehicle washers and equipment cleaners (28%); brick masons (37%) and bartenders (42%).

Not long ago, while providing an in-service training to teachers at their district headquarters, I noticed the audience making such an assumption *en masse*. I asked how many teachers the school district employed. Four hundred was the response. I then asked what percentage of them could be considered as working under highly stressful conditions. "Almost all of them," was the reply (a statistic which I do not doubt). "So, if stress causes alcoholism, what you're saying is that the district employs 400 alcoholics?" Obviously, the teachers saw the hole in their reasoning.

Certainly, stress will have a great impact on a person who desires to maintain a program of abstinence. Those who go to support groups such as Alcoholics Anonymous notice particular attention is paid to preventing or managing stress. "Think of the acronym HALT," they are repeatedly advised. "Don't get too (H)ungry, (A)ngry, (L)onely or (T)ired." To do so will threaten your sobriety by placing undue stress on yourself. Using a tool like HALT is good advice; but let no one believe that being in a HALT situation makes a person alcoholic.

Trauma

Many seek treatment for trauma which occurred during childhood or adolescence. If they are alcoholic, they often believe their alcoholism is a direct result of the trauma. But does everyone who experiences trauma become alcoholic? The answer, of course, is "no." In fact, couldn't it just as easily be said that *alcoholism can cause trauma?* Talk to people who treat abused clients every day and they'll admit to noticing a "chicken or egg" relationship. In other words, they are often unsure if the alcoholism contributed to the abuse or if the abuse fueled the alcoholism.

Again, if your loved one believes that alcoholism is caused by trauma then she might be tempted to think: "I am an alcoholic because I was abused and therefore alcoholism therapy must wait until I get trauma counseling." In the recovery process, the first priority is to get sober. Then, and only then, can the emotional scar of trauma be dealt with.

Lack of adequate coping skills

It wouldn't be surprising if some of the coping skills your alcoholic learned as a child are inappropriate for adulthood; or any appropriate coping skills he previously possessed may have atrophied under the progression of alcoholism.

Childhood, for many, is a troubled, perhaps traumatic, time. Kids trust adults (parents, relatives, coaches and teachers) to meet their needs while they busy themselves with school and play. Often, children get a front-row seat for a traumatic display of domestic violence or a messy divorce and child custody case. They may be victimized sexually or emotionally by a family member to the degree that profound issues of trust and abandonment are laid down for life. They may be placed on the proverbial pedestal which is an often-unacknowledged form of child abuse. Each child learns to develop coping skills that remove them physically or mentally from such stress and trauma. Some cope by assuming responsibility for running the household; some become runners who devise 101 ways to exit a tense situation. Others — at the first sign of friction — grab a thick book, take it somewhere and stick their nose in it until the yelling stops. Still others continually get sick, act out, experiment with mood-altering chemicals, disassociate, fantasize, become comedians, look for others to fix them, succumb to religiosity or mutilate themselves (the list goes on).

What happens to kids who coped with adolescence by running? They continue to run as adults. Children who coped by isolating often seek counseling as adults because they can't stop isolating. Clients who coped by getting sick find they cannot stay off pain medication or out of hospitals. And women who coped by taking care of everyone in the family often become health care providers who nurse patients from 8 to 5 and nurse yet another in a series of shiftless men until they go back to work in the morning.

As a therapist who on a daily basis heard terrible stories of what clients had to deal with, I so often wished I could have presented each one with a trophy etched with the words: "Congratulations — you got through childhood!" Along with a written, gilt-edged guarantee that the same coping skill which made childhood tolerable would be inappropriate for adulthood.

And that's the cruel joke about coping skills; those that successfully get one through a traumatic childhood often turn adulthood into a disaster. Adulthood is far more complex than childhood. Being grown-up carries with it lots of responsibility — children, spouses, aged parents, careers, money woes and career disappointments. Poor coping skills learned in childhood will be inadequate to solve such problems.

Expecting poor coping skills to carry over into adulthood is so common that when a client shares a complaint, an observant therapist will most often hear how poorly she learned to cope as a child. Conversely, men who describe how they coped with childhood will unwittingly tip off a therapist as to the extent of their current problem. Much of the resulting therapeutic relationship will be applied toward teaching such clients to unlearn what they once learned so well.

Loss and grief

Loss takes many forms. The death of parents and other loved ones; failure to conceive children; removal of children from the home by state and local authorities; abandonment of loved ones because of the choices one makes in alcoholism; throwing away life opportunities because of drinking.

Alcoholism causes loss because it kills hope, potential, ambition, opportunity, dreams, promise, goals, self-esteem, not to mention millions of brain cells. It robs its victims of short- and long-term memory, muscle tone, beauty, creativity, joy and youth. It kills marriages, engagements, parent/child relationships and, ultimately, life itself. To follow alcoholism down its "wrong roads" (as Goethe put it) is to understand profound loss.

Grief is how we deal with loss. But grief and the consumption of alcohol are — like oil and water — incompatible. The relationship between grief and alcoholism is ironic, if not diabolical — *alcoholism produces loss and prevents grief*. It matters not if an alcoholic goes to the funeral of a loved one and appears to grieve; she may weep loudly and be the most histrionic person at the wake; but if she is drinking, she isn't grieving.

Grief is a process; there's a beginning and an end to it — as Dr. Elisabeth Kübler-Ross delineated so well in her book *On Death and Dying*. First there's denial, anger, an attempt to bargain with God, depression and finally acceptance. All the steps of grief — the grief process — must be experienced. Needless to say, this requires a sober mind.

Let's now imagine that our alcoholic has been drinking for the last 30 years. During that time, he's lost to death both parents, a few Army buddies, some co-workers and a few favorite aunts and uncles. Plus, he realizes that he never lived up to his own potential and thus his dreams have died. This person now chooses to recover, seeks counseling and becomes a member of Alcoholics Anonymous. He's glad to be sober and he's working on himself with the aid of a sponsor, but he can't for the life of him figure out why he keeps thinking and dreaming about his parents, old Army buddies and other family members. He's also stymied as to why he cries over his family photograph album so much that the concern of family members is elicited.

It can't be grief, he'll argue. "My mom and dad died a long time ago." But it is. He soaked his brain in alcohol the last three decades and didn't grieve a thing. All that stored-up grief is now finally available. That's what makes it so important for recovery to be done in a support group. When the last drink is drunk, that grief barrier goes down and all that pent-up sorrow will soon start pounding at the door. He'll learn that dealing with such grief will be a high priority in treatment and that it won't be accomplished in a short period of time.

Victimization

At the level of personal recovery, victimization (powerlessness over everything) is a major roadblock to chemical freedom. Breathes there an alcoholic who, prior to climbing on a bar stool or buying a bottle, hasn't first perceived herself as a victim? For most, it's a prerequisite for getting drunk. "No one understands me; I've never been given a break; it seems the whole world is against me," and so on. Or, the alcoholic may perceive that he's a victim of himself: "I'm not good enough; I'm not handsome enough; I'm not smart enough." If Shakespeare said that hunger is the best sauce, then surely resentments are the best chasers.

Is it any wonder why those in Twelve-Step groups spend much more time identifying and surrendering such resentments than they do discussing alcohol? They know that holding on to resentments will sooner or later get them back to feeling victimized and then relapse is inevitable.

Lack of money

Once in a blue moon an alcoholic shows up for treatment with money or insurance. Most often, however, they have squandered their money, had it stolen from them or, in the case of cocaine, they've shoved it up their nose. Alcoholics go through money like water, but it's not always for booze. So often it's for breath mints, eye drops and antacids — items to get them through the hangover period. Yes, these are penny-ante items, but over a 10-20-year drinking career they can certainly add up. In fact, one highly-instructive treatment exercise has the alcoholic adding up all the money he's spent on his disease during his "drinking career." Large amounts of money are also spent for attorneys and DUI fines and, on occasion, to pay off a bookie or a loan shark. The amount of money one can spend on street drugs like cocaine boggles the mind. One former patient whose cocaine usage began in Salt Lake City bottomed out in Phoenix and admitted to me that without exaggeration, he'd spent $50,000 in two years.

Poor accounting

Another choice alcoholics must make is whether to drink or account for their money. Most often their accounting suffers. During blackouts they write checks they don't remember writing to people they don't remember meeting for things they can easily live without. They remove money from automated teller machines without writing down the amount. They max out their credit cards in a vain attempt to buy the love of their spouse or children who have been too long ignored to be mollified by material things. Even if an alcoholic were to come into treatment with money, chances are good he won't have a clue as to where it is.

Poor health and dental hygiene

Another choice your alcoholic must make is whether to drink or take care of his body and teeth. Rare is the inebriate who chooses the latter. There are reasons for this. Many alcoholics either don't have the money for medical/dental care or they have it but prefer to spend it on alcohol. And the reader must admit that to make and keep doctor and dentist appointments — and pay for them — a life must have some semblance of order. Newly-sober alcoholics have often shied away from medical help for so long that there's a good chance they'll spend a few days of their newly-found sobriety in a hospital for some long-ignored malady (hypertension, obesity, heavy smoking). This leads to the oft-heard crack that "I never got sick until I sobered up." Alcoholics fear that the doctor will stick a needle into them and all of their secrets will pour out. Or that they will be handed a specimen cup to pass what may prove to be a urine stream of consciousness. So sure of this are most alcoholics that they won't even think about a doctor until it's too late. Interestingly enough, with more and more diagnostic tools available to doctors, the alcoholics are correct. Today, any doctor can draw blood and pretty well tell if a patient has physical symptoms of alcoholism.

Failure to pay taxes

If you ever want to startle members of an alcoholism support group, stand before them and mention delinquent taxes. One great example of *a priori* knowledge is that any gaggle of alcoholics will include many who have failed to pay taxes for a long, long time. It's those pesky choices again. Constant fear of the IRS helps keep the alcoholic stuck as he can't conceive of getting sober just to spend the rest of his days in prison. AA's Twelve Steps provides a vehicle for removing this millstone in the form of taking initiative, admitting the problem, working out a payment plan with the IRS and forking over hard dollars for the first of many payments. This is called a "financial amends."

Gambling debts

Alcoholism has its own counterpart to peanut butter and jelly, Burns and Allen, coffee and cream. It's the relationship between drinking and gambling — two habits guaranteed to turn any relationship into cornmeal mush. Those aware of losing their financial base become suckers for get-rich-quick schemes and with a gambling casino seemingly on every block these days, they don't have far to go. So severe can this problem be — especially if the alcoholic is a pathological or cross-addicted gambler — that often the alcoholic's first intervention is done not by a family member but by the IRS or a loan shark. Remember, it may take an alcoholic months or years to lose a house; a gambler can do it in five minutes.

Lifestyle

The late Beat Generation writer William S. Burroughs, in the prologue to his 1953 autobiography *Junky*, rightly says that "Junk [drugs] is not a kick. It is a way of life." Every therapist has no doubt encountered a walking personification of this edict in the form of the do-rag wearing, hip, slick, cool, multi-tattooed, jailhouse-bullshit-talking street hustler who swears he wants to get and stay clean but is doomed to failure because he can't change his all-pervasive junkie lifestyle. For a therapist to warn this person against hanging around the old neighborhood is a joke; this person's life is dominated by slippery playgrounds and slippery people. It's like asking a fish not to go back to the water.

Alcoholism, too, is a lifestyle. The composite alcoholic passes out every night while others are going to sleep, and "comes to" each morning while others are waking up. He swears off alcohol every morning and tries to get through the day without being too enfeebled by a hangover. Feeling better around 4 pm, he says "one more drink won't hurt me" and takes his regular seat at the bar after work where he holds court until 10 pm. Picking up a six-pack or two for the road, he careens home where he spends the wee hours of the morning knocking back beers.

It doesn't help for him to get exercise — all his golf or bowling buddies drink as much or more than he does. Those so-called "service organizations" where he spends Friday nights, Saturday nights and Sunday afternoons may contribute to charities but all too often function as drinking academies. And vacations? Most alcoholics view vacations as an opportunity to see if booze tastes as good on the East Coast as it does on the West.

During treatment, it often dawns on alcoholics that what they think is only a bottle problem is also a lifestyle problem. Getting abstinent for a week or two is the easy part; wholesale rearrangement of their living environment to support their abstinence will be mighty tough sledding.

Prostitution of values

This word conjures up an image of a heroin addict walking the streets in skimpy clothing. But there's another side of prostitution that many recovering alcoholics (especially women) must deal with once they get sober. That's the guilt of using their bodies to get their needs met while drinking.

Short of money for alcohol? Ask a guy to bring over enough booze for a two-person party. Can't make the rent payment? A couple of meaningful one-night stands with an old boyfriend and the rent's paid for another month. Car need fixing? Every woman knows a guy who can fix it and if he stays over to (as Shakespeare says) "make the beast with two backs" who's the wiser? I've had many female clients who said, "Whoever provides me with alcohol or other drugs, be it man or woman, can have me — I just don't care."

The contract between a hooker and her john is explicit. The contract between an alcoholic woman and the men who meet her financial needs may be unspoken to the point of unawareness. Later, when she recovers and her memories become available, she'll need a formal support group to deal with the fact that alcoholics — men and women — habitually violate their personal code of morals.

Mental health problems

Those with both mental health problems and alcoholism are said to have a dual diagnosis. Some of the most common mental illnesses afflicting alcoholics include major depression, bipolar disorder, antisocial personality disorder, narcissism, borderline personality disorder, anxiety, phobia and panic disorder.

Managing a patient with a dual diagnosis is challenging. Some do well in therapy circles; others do not. Some contribute to group cohesiveness; others disrupt it. If the focus is entirely on the alcoholism, a therapist may miss a critical relapse trigger or confuse delusional thinking with common denial. Likewise, if a therapist places too much emphasis on a mental health diagnosis the alcoholic may milk the therapist for unneeded medications or demand constant recognition of his or her "uniqueness." Constantly reminding an alcoholic that he has mental health issues may also contribute to an attitude of hopelessness: "It's all too much, I'll never make it."

Central to the issue of providing treatment to the dually-diagnosed patient is the management of medication. Each patient must understand that if they are prescribed meds, they must take them — even if they are feeling good. And, yes, people with bipolar disorders must learn to medicate their *mania* as well as their depression. Psychiatrists must learn not to diagnose a patient until he's been sober long enough for a clear picture of his mental health to emerge. CD nurses must learn not to reward a patient's "med-seeking" behaviors and AA old-timers must learn to practice their code of patience and tolerance with fellow members who happen to need psychoactive agents.

Genetics

While it obviously can't be said to result from his disease (as the prior list of symptoms can), the genetic make-up of your alcoholic is certainly a major contributing factor. Therapists have long noticed that alcoholism seems to run in certain biological families. Most often the alcoholic will admit during the intake procedure that, yes, her grandparents, father or mother were heavy drinkers. But beware: this is an inexact science. Often an alcoholic will tell how his family was a stranger to alcohol while his social-drinking wife will disclose the frustration of growing up in an alcoholic family.

In 1990, one researcher pinpointed a gene which he noticed was largely present in the genetic material of autopsied alcoholics who had died of their disease. This received quite a lot of publicity (and yes, resulted in a few calls to NCADD/Phoenix from worried spouses asking if something could be done with their husband's genes to make them stop drinking!). I suspect that this gene might be the first of many. But it's important to remember that genes do not cause alcoholism — one receives from genes a *tendency* toward alcoholism.

Other candidates

Other candidates for the cause of alcoholism — sin (moral model), lack of will-power (character model), physiological necessity (biological model), repressed emotional conflict (psychoanalytic model), poor role models (social model), or a natural reaction to a cold, unfeeling universe (existential model) — are fascinating to ponder but don't work in the trenches, i.e., face-to-face with a therapist, in a circle of chairs, in a treatment center or in a support group. Each becomes trivial and irrelevant when a demoralized alcoholic walks into a therapist's office and closes the door.

Much more down-to-earth models such as alienation from a Higher Power (spiritual model), irrational thinking (cognitive model), poor coping skills (behavior model) and repressed feelings (affective model) have been found to be "usable" and are the focus of most treatment centers and AA.

To summarize

The causes of alcoholism, one might say, are *global* (if not cosmic); alcoholism treatment and recovery are *local*. An alcoholic will not be cured if you reduce his shame, give him money, solve his medical problems, fix his teeth, patch up his credit, pay his taxes, call off the loan sharks, cure his depression or make him stop violating his moral code. All you'll have is a happy, healthy alcoholic with money in the bank, swell teeth, another year without an IRS audit and unbroken knee caps. This is why trained counselors don't fall for excuses from people who seek alcoholism treatment and then try to take them on a wild goose chase regarding secondary issues. As a loved one, you shouldn't either.

Chapter 4

Don't Look for Logic

When you walk into an alcoholism clinic you've walked into a logic-free zone. There should be signs over the doorway announcing: "Abandon all logic ye who enter here."

The ghost of Jacob Marley in Dickens' *A Christmas Carol* is a terrifying fellow who's dispatching the sins of a parsimonious life by dragging around — to great theatrical effect — heavy chains that announce his every move. Likewise, if you happen to love an alcoholic, you might be dragging around your own heavy chain — figuratively speaking. The difference is that Marley's Ghost was aware of his chains; you may not be. All you know is that something heavy keeps dragging you down. If you fail to cast off this burden, you will continue searching for something you're not going to find and your entry into recovery will be further delayed.

To carry this chain is to search for a link between logic and alcoholism. Nothing at all wrong with a little intellectual excursion into human nature or psychology. But continuing to ask why a perfectly intelligent person seems hell-bent on killing himself with alcohol will add lines to your face and leave you with few answers. You might as well ask why enablers — in the face of constant and overwhelming defeat — continue their enabling.

Alcoholics who recover through AA know that the word "insanity" is defined there as "Continuing to do the same action while expecting different results." The alcoholic continues to drink, always thinking, "Maybe it will be different this time." Loved ones like you, too, join the rush to insanity by searching for logic after having failed the last 800 times. "I'll ask again and maybe this time I'll find the answer."

You: I just don't get it. She's so intelligent; he's so talented; they both have such a wonderful family; their earning potential is tremendous; their house is so nice; she's up for advancement; he made the football team; she's on the Dean's List and the Pompom Squad; their whole future is ahead of them — so why don't they stop drinking?
Counselor: How long have you been asking this question?
You: Fifteen years.
Counselor: How close are you to finding the answer?
You: Further than ever.

An alcoholism clinic is not the place to start looking for logic. If that's your goal, go to an engineering office — they've got logic to burn. Talk to a scientist, a surgeon or an airline pilot. They deal with logic all the time.

But when you walk into an alcoholism clinic you've walked into a logic-free zone. There should be signs over the doorway announcing: "Abandon all logic ye who enter here." The reason, of course, is that alcoholism and all other forms of chemical dependency have nothing to do with logic. The conflict comes because almost everything else in society does. Logic must be used to get a car from point A to point B; buildings must be built to conform with logical methods of construction; if you're planning to work around computers, you'd better make logic your friend.

Loved ones and concerned persons always seek treatment asking "why" questions — "Why doesn't he drink like my other children?" "Why does he continue to do this after being in three treatment centers?" The question "why," when examined, anticipates an answer, presumes logic and reveals a "cosmic" nature. That is to say that the answer may well be off in the cosmos somewhere.

It's not unheard of to live life in the absence of logic. We don't know where in the universe we are; we don't know what happens after death; it's still up in the air as to whether the universe will expand forever or contract; and we don't know why people kill each other. Americans don't even know why Jerry Lewis is idolized in France.

It is easy to forget that alcoholism and logic are polar opposites. Thus, it's possible to have this sort of conversation:

Client: I've learned from my last DUI that I have a drinking and driving problem. From now on, I'm going to make sure when I start drinking that I don't get into a car.

Counselor: That's a noble and very logical thought, but are you in the habit of drinking for logic? Is sound thinking and rational judgment what you're really looking for when you take a drink?

Client: (Smiles) Not exactly. I just like the buzz.

Counselor: What happens when you get the buzz?

Client: I get goofy, sort of funny in the head.

Counselor: What I hear you saying is that you don't drink alcohol to achieve rational judgment.

Client: I guess not.

Counselor: So are you surprised that rational judgment says goodbye when alcohol enters your system?

Certainly, the client will have a history of promising to give someone else the keys when he drinks. He might even rehearse how he'll surrender his car keys to friends after just two beers. He might have a long talk with the hostess and enlist her to demand his keys after the party. However, something always happens to thwart that effort — he starts drinking. Then his mind gets messed up and all his best laid plans go right out the window.

The same thing happens to those who learn about safe sex in order to avoid the virus that causes AIDS. Courses are taken and literature is read. Safe sex techniques are memorized to the point where our person in question could teach the course herself. "These techniques are quite logical and well thought out," she might think to herself and indeed they are. To be effective, though, the practitioners must be rational. Far too many people learn about safe sex, start drinking and wind up in bed having unprotected sex with a stranger.

Trying to use logic to deal with alcoholism won't work partly because logic has to do with the brain's frontal lobes where cognitive functions lie. The alcoholic, however, seems to be governed by the much older reptilian brain. In other words, the appeal to logic never works because the sole object of drinking is to impair or disconnect that logical function. In my experience, I've never heard anyone say they drink to "transform my cognitive chaos into cognitive clarity." Quite the opposite. I've also never seen anyone seek treatment and, in a manner reminiscent of Star Trek's Mr. Spock, proclaim, "I've given it plenty of thought; I've read all I can; I've run a special computer program on this and I'm here for treatment." To the contrary, everyone comes in figuratively stabbed in the heart because they disappointed themselves or someone they love very much.

Back in 1990, a Phoenix attorney made an appointment with me to discuss the drinking problem of his niece. After we greeted each other, he asked if it were possible for him to take notes. I urged him to do so and he pulled from his pouch a yellow legal pad. As the session progressed, I began to perceive that he was composing a legal brief as doubtless he had done many times in his career. Was he convinced that he could help his niece by proving that her drinking wasn't logical? I then did what is known to therapists as a "here and now" and asked him whether my hunch was correct. It was and we spent the remainder of the session discussing why alcoholism doesn't respond to logic and discussing realistic steps that could be taken toward getting her help.

In Chapter 7 on *Formally Intervening*, I will tell you about a tried and true method of getting someone into treatment even if he doesn't want to go. The process will require certain tasks but determining "why" the target of concern is alcoholic is not one of them. Likewise, those who read the book *Alcoholics Anonymous* will not find a chapter entitled, "Into Thinking" or "Into Asking Why." They will, however, find a most helpful chapter entitled "Into Action."

Acceptance of the fact that your loved one is alcoholic is your only true option. If you spend your energy working on yourself rather than trying to connect drinking with logic, you'll be that much farther along. The answer is to stop asking "why" and start asking *"how* can I find the help that I need?"

Chapter 5

It's Not Social Drinking

Concerned family members often fail to understand how a therapist can speak of alcoholism as a disease and, in the same breath, talk about choices. How can a person with a disease have choices?

Most adult Americans (if they drink at all) are true social drinkers. Chances are high that you are too. If so, the following description of how social drinkers behave around alcohol should describe you to a T:

Social drinkers sip their drinks, drink them one at a time, rarely overindulge, leave full bottles in the home bar so long they get dusty, forget to drink, pour out a drink when the ice melts, fret about the color and "bouquet" of their wine, split beers with someone else, won't drink if they've already brushed their teeth, might not refill a drink if they spill it and basically drink only to be social. They don't get arrested because of their drinking and they remember who they went to bed with the night before. They can predict their actions when they drink, they don't break promises when drinking, they don't drink just for effect, they don't swear off alcohol, they don't push drinks on you, they don't mix you unusually strong drinks and they don't notice if you're not drinking.

Your alcoholic probably views this behavior as strange and he'll tend to dismiss you as one of life's little mysteries. He'll never understand you but will pretend to be a social drinker to get you off his back. He might say, "Yes, I'm a social drinker; every time I get drunk there are others around." (It's interesting to ask him if anyone else was drinking. So often, the answer is "no.") Or he might believe that social drinking is akin to getting drunk only five times a year.

Your alcoholic describing her concept of social drinking will sound like someone from Lapland describing life in Bolivia. She'll be unable to believe that most social drinkers care little about the alcohol they drink. Or she may be dubious about your ability to stop at one — thinking perhaps you retreat to the restroom on occasion and knock back a few on the sly. Here's a list of things that are considered to be symptoms of the disease of alcoholism. And keep in mind that true social drinkers don't display these symptoms:

Denial

Alcoholism is a strange disease in that it's essentially a disease of denial. Further, many say it's a disease that tries to tell its sufferers that they don't have a disease. Dr. Elisabeth Kübler-Ross, the mother of the modern hospice movement, has written extensively about the role denial plays in terminal diseases such as certain cancers. But that denial is slight compared to that which plagues alcoholics. I believe that if cancer patients experienced denial of the same magnitude as alcoholics, very few would ever seek treatment.

By denial, I don't mean rushing out of your house, grabbing the first person you meet and asking, "Are you an alcoholic?" When he says "no," you proclaim, "Well that sounds like denial and that means you're an alcoholic." What this chapter is concerned with is the person who, in the face of severe symptoms, DUI arrests, broken marriages, and a long history of detoxification and treatment, denies having a problem. That's pathological denial and it happens all the time.

Denial is complicated by the fact that everyone can do it. A spouse is in denial when she says to someone, "Sure he drinks a lot, but he's under heavy stress at work." Likewise, children join the denial when they provide a cover story for mom who doesn't show up at a family reunion. Church members, too, can deny the obvious by saying, "Sister is a good Christian; she tithes and comes to choir practice every Wednesday — you're trying to tell me she's a drunk?" Employers and fellow workers join the chorus when they consistently cover for an employee, saying, "He'll be just fine when the Civic Center Project is finished."

No one truly knows why denial is such a pervasive symptom of alcoholism. It could be social/ethnic/cultural factors or the lingering stigma of drunkenness. It could be that the brain of the alcoholic is impaired to the extent that the sufferer is unaware when jail or death are imminent. It could be that the impairment of a loved one brings issues of shame and co-dependency to the fore. It could be that Freud was right when he listed denial along with many other quite normal "ego defense mechanisms." It could be the insidiousness of the disease that gives the alcoholic plenty of time to perfect excuses. It could be a form of mild dissociation. Or T. S. Eliot could have nailed denial when he wrote that, "Human kind cannot bear very much reality."

Make no mistake, just as the disease of alcoholism is progressive, so too is denial. At the beginning of a drinker's "career," enough denial must be available to handle, say, three or four beers. At the end, when vodka is being drunk right out of the bottle, when the DUIs start showing up, the denial must have progressed enough to veil that kind of sickness. Do social drinkers exhibit denial? No. Alcohol has such a slight effect on their lives that denial never enters the picture.

Tolerance

Want to know another thing social drinkers don't do? They don't display tolerance. Tolerance, so to speak, is when the price of admission keeps going up; when it takes more and more alcohol to achieve a desired effect (or less of an effect is achieved by drinking a constant amount). The signature of a social drinker is that over months, years or even decades, her consumption of alcohol does not increase. Social drinkers will begin drinking in 1952 with a daily can of beer and end up at the year 2010 drinking a like amount.

Contrast that with the alcoholic who quickly notices an interesting effect. He drinks a beer with the boys and gets giggly, goofy, sleepy or any of those other effects of alcohol which sound like members of the Seven Dwarfs. This act is pleasurable and, as pleasurable acts often are, is soon repeated. Along the way, however, the alcoholic soon notices that in order to achieve the original pleasurable effect or "high," two beers must be consumed. And then three, a six-pack, two six-packs and perhaps some distilled spirits to wash it all down. Before he knows it, lots of alcohol is being drunk and the original high is not even reachable anymore. The drinker continues consuming, however, partly because he can't remember life without alcohol.

Alcoholics are often proud of the fact that they can "drink everyone else under the table." Why are many people (mostly males, it seems) so proud of this tolerance? It could be a macho thing where the ability to tolerate booze is likened to an ever-increasing ability to bench press weights or satisfy a sexual partner. Whatever the reason, this is a major symptom of the disease of alcoholism and it's nothing to boast about.

One word more to the spouse of an alcoholic who notices this ever-increasing tolerance followed by a drastic drop in consumption. (Keep in mind I'm not talking about a person surprising you by drinking only one beer in an effort to control his drinking). If you observe a loved one consuming up to a quart of distilled spirits a day, or a case of beer, then suddenly getting drunk on a single beer, it usually means extreme liver damage and high time for an overdue visit to the doctor. This type of *reverse tolerance* is not a good sign.

Loss of control

We've already discussed this aspect in Chapter 2, *It's a Disease*, when we clinically defined an alcoholic *as a person with a pathological problem who, once he chooses to start, finds it extremely difficult to stop drinking.* This loss of control doesn't come from simply looking at a bottle; it appears when it's poured down the throat. Trying to control the use of alcohol is a symptom of alcoholism. Our friend the social drinker doesn't do this. Attempts to control her drinking are as foreign to her as Esperanto.

But our alcoholic will try everything to control it. He'll try switching brands, going from bourbon and Scotch to gin and vodka; he'll go back to beer then give the old "white wine maintenance program" a try. He'll start drinking at a different time of day; start using a shot glass again; tell his bartender "just give me five drinks tonight and no more — even if I beg you." In areas of the country where alcohol is not sold on Sundays (is there still such a place?) alcoholics will buy only enough alcohol to last through Saturday night, thus ensuring (they hope) sobriety on Sunday and the rest of the week.

Want to know how an alcoholic can capture the complete attention of an alcoholism counselor? Simply by using the word "weekend" when she describes her drinking. Why do you suppose someone would relegate all her drinking to the weekend — more specifically to Friday and Saturday nights? Might it have something to do with trying to control her drinking? Alcoholics, after some bad experiences with hangovers on Monday mornings (not to mention angry or suspicious bosses) quickly learn to stay away from drinking until they can get plowed without interfering with work (with families, certainly, and with children, but inebriates are funny about jobs!) So they live for Friday nights, get blasted, stumble around on Saturday morning, get drunk again on Saturday night and then somehow get it together for Monday and the rest of the work week.

Our friends the social drinkers — do they limit their alcohol use to weekends? Certainly not. Those who don't have to worry about controlling their drinking can drink any day. If they want a glass of Chianti with their pasta tonight they may do so with impunity.

Concerned family members often fail to understand (and who can blame them?) how a therapist can speak of alcoholism as a disease and, in the same breath, talk about choices. How can a person with a disease have choices?

An alcoholic doesn't have a choice as to whether he has the disease. That's a done deal. Neither does he have a choice as to the *second*, third, fourth and 20th drinks (the so-called "drink drinks") — those are explained by the fact that he has a physical disease called alcoholism. Those drinks are a given. However, he may *choose* not to activate his disease by taking the first drink (the so-called "think drink"). That's the only control — the only true choice — he has. Thus it may be possible to say that an alcoholic is not a person who consistently drinks, but a person who consistently *chooses* to start drinking again.

If they know they can't stop, why do they start? Good question. In fact, it's such a good question that it's been the subject of every meeting of Alcoholics Anonymous since 1935. AA is not concerned at all about the second, third, fourth or fifth drinks. It is *very concerned*, however, with the first one — "You can't get drunk if you don't take that first drink" is they way they tell it. "It's not the caboose of the train that runs over you — it's the engine." Alcoholics most often list the following as reasons why they take the "think" drink: anger, fear, stress, unresolved resentments, poor management of leisure time, inability to identify the energy of those around them, lack of contact with recovering alcoholics, spiritual malaise, forgetting the last drink and generally, having nothing in their lives (like a methodical program of recovery) to prevent relapse.

Inability to predict consequences

Social drinkers always seem to know what they're going to do once they take a drink. They're going to get sleepy, read a magazine or get called to dinner. No surprises, nothing new. (Some of my more creative clients ask, in their best existential fashion, "Well, can anyone really predict what's going to happen to them in this life?" No they can't. The argument here, however, is can *you* predict what *you're* going to do when *you* start drinking?)

So, what happens when your loved one drinks? Does he say something suggestive to the boss's spouse? Does she get stopped by police? Does she wake up with strangers who may or may not be HIV-positive? Does he break promises to himself and others? Does he shoot those he loves in a blackout and wake up in jail? Does she run over and kill the neighbor kids on her way home from a toot? True alcoholics roll the dice every time they take a drink.

Subtle withdrawal

Because of Hollywood films such as *The Lost Weekend, The Man With the Golden Arm, Days of Wine & Roses, Rush* and *Trainspotters,* millions of movie goers over the last 50 years have gotten a pretty good look at what withdrawal from alcohol and other drugs is like. Actors are shown writhing on beds, bats are depicted as coming out of walls, and so on. All too true in some cases but Hollywood may have left the impression that all withdrawal is like that. It isn't. To be sure, withdrawal from anything fully depended upon by the central nervous system is serious. Putting the plug in the jug for many will result in the classic signs of withdrawal: shakes, seizures and hallucinations. It's best to do that kind of withdrawal with medical assistance.

This dramatic image of withdrawal that Hollywood has shown us over the years may lead alcoholics to think that if they don't exhibit such drama, they must not have a problem. However, there is another type of withdrawal that all alcoholics have noticed — and because it has nothing to do with high drama won't be coming to a Multiplex Cinema near you. This is a very subtle kind of withdrawal: A man goes on vacation with his family, stops for the evening at a motel and starts thinking about drinking. He goes to the local supermarket and walks up and down the aisles searching in vain for beer, wine or distilled spirits. Confused as to why there seems to be none, he asks a manager who informs him: "Sir, we don't sell the stuff; this is a dry county."

Frightened and angry, our alcoholic returns to the motel and in the general direction of his wife, rants and raves, saying things like, "What kind of a one-horse, jerk-water burg is this?" The alcoholic is clearly agitated at the thought of spending a restless night far away from home without a drink. Other examples of this kind of subtle withdrawal include: looking forward to the spiked punch bowl at a wedding only to find out that it's Southern Baptist not Roman

Catholic; becoming angry that your host and hostess have already run out of beer or wine and it's only 8 pm; being aware that you have a major presentation at work tomorrow and finding yourself angry that you don't dare have a drink tonight. Needless to say, social drinkers don't do this.

Notice that while these alcoholics might not be going into classic withdrawal, there's still that agitation — that restlessness. I submit that this type of mild withdrawal should also be considered as a symptom of alcoholism. Doubtless, your alcoholic, while boasting that he's neither shaken nor seizured, is keeping you in the dark about all the times he's exhibited anger, irritation or restlessness when unable to obtain and consume alcohol.

Broken promises

Breaking promises, while not as easy to observe as tolerance or withdrawal, is considered a real symptom of alcoholism. One doesn't get very far down the road to problem drinking without reneging on commitments. Broken promises come in two types: promises broken to others and to yourself.

Examples of the former include the time your alcoholic promised to be there for your birthday or your child's Little League game. He knows he missed it last year, but this year he's good for it. First however, he's going to go see this old friend and they just might have a beer or two. "So start getting ready, put on that new dress and I'll be back at five."

Examples of the latter are legion: "Only real alcoholics drink in the afternoon, so you'll never catch me doing that. Okay, I'm drinking in the afternoon, but only real alcoholics drink in the morning. Okay, I'm drinking in the morning but at least you'll never catch me drinking and driving. OOPS! I'm drinking and driving, but at least the kids aren't with me. Uh oh, now I'm drinking and driving with the kids in the car." This occurs over so much time that the alcoholic isn't even aware that it's happening.

This is not to say that alcoholics enjoy breaking promises or even purposely do so. Indeed, such things leave them with guilt and as much curiosity as to why they do them as you have. They just can't help it once they choose to start drinking.

Blackouts

Blackouts (alcohol-induced amnesia) are not hard to understand. When the brain is flooded with alcohol, it's forced to make choices. The brain understands that it must concentrate on functions vital to life (heart beat, metabolism, respiration, etc.), so it inventories and shuts down what a person doesn't need — *memory* for instance. Thus, conscious choice remains available but a person loses the ability to remember what's happening. Make no mistake, once that memory is shut off during a blackout, it cannot be retrieved. Neither hypnosis nor sodium pentothol will bring it back.

The term blackout is often seized upon by the alcoholic to mitigate an embarrassing or felonious action: "I don't know why I molested my daughter; I must have been in a blackout." To the contrary, a blackout doesn't cause you to do things you would not normally do.

Alcoholics don't always have blackouts, but those who do often have lots of stories which point out how much we rely on short-term memory. Like the time one said she came out of a blackout in a job interview. She had been doing rather well, but all of a sudden didn't know those in front of her nor did she remember why she was there. Or the guy who took a drink in Alaska and came out of a blackout in Dallas without having any idea how he got there. Another classic had to do with a now-deceased flight instructor from an Air Force base near Phoenix who led a squadron to morning target practice at the Air Force Gunnery Range south of Gila Bend, Arizona. The pilot came out of his blackout in inverted flight and didn't remember assembling his squadron, briefing it, taking off or starting his target runs. When he finally got back to the base, he was severely rattled and in true alcoholic fashion, spent the rest of the afternoon in the Officer's Club — drinking alcohol.

Comments from others

Your alcoholic won't get too far in his disease before someone mentions his drinking. This begins casually: "Wow, you sure drank that beer fast!" Then the mentions get more serious: "You aren't planning to drink at the party tonight are you?" Then things really get severe: "Mr. Jones, I'm sentencing you to six months in jail." Or, "I love you but the kids and I can't deal with the way you drink anymore."

People who mention the way an alcoholic drinks will include parents, teachers, clergy, old girlfriends, drinking buddies, current wives, ex-husbands, lovers, co-workers, supervisors, doctors, newspaper columnists, *Hard Copy* reporters, the police, judges, prison guards, psych nurses and finally, morticians.

At first, mentions are few. Finally, when the drinking becomes out of control, it's a chorus. Does this happen to you? Of course not. True social drinkers go all their lives without anyone mentioning how they drink.

Swearing off

This classic symptom of alcoholism (promising to quit or taper off) is usually such a systemic part of the alcoholic that she's barely aware of it. "After all, doesn't everyone swear off once in a while?" she'll ask. There's a thousand and one ways to swear off alcohol — they all seem so honest and so full of promise. In fact, this may be the only symptom of alcoholism that is applauded and rewarded by families and friends.

There's the person who swears off every day or every Monday morning. There's the person who swears off to himself, to close friends, to large groups or on TV talk shows.

Remember that in order to swear off, an original problem with alcohol must be encountered. Otherwise, why would a person ever do it? People don't just walk down the street and suddenly announce, "I think I'll just promise to quit alcohol." Not without a fairly strong reason they don't. So what would cause the kind of problem that would lead your alcoholic to swear off? How about his inability to handle alcohol without getting fired, getting DUIs and hurting the ones he loves?

Swearing off is usually done under the mistaken notion that alcoholism goes away once you put a little time between your last and your next drink. Hardly any alcoholic swears off without thinking to herself: "I'll go back to it after the heat's off."

I believe the length of time for which an alcoholic decides to swear off is directionally proportional to the severity of the current dilemma. A young person who misses a sporting event because of a hangover might vow to stop for a couple of days while a person who's watched spouse and children walk out will swear off forever.

As a social drinker, do you ever swear off? Of course not. There's never an original problem to merit swearing off. Swearing off is not a symptom of new-found maturity; it's a sign of alcoholism.

Drinking for effect

Call it "getting a buzz," "getting high," "getting loaded" or whatever, alcoholics drink solely for the effect it gives them. That is, until they go so far down on the Jellinek Chart that their search for euphoria is replaced by their need to keep detoxification symptoms at bay.

Often, in a clinical setting, a person will announce, in all innocence, that "I don't drink very much but sure, I really like to get that buzz." And that's the problem — getting that buzz — that euphoria. Nothing wrong with a little euphoria, it's just that a bottle of alcohol means to the alcoholic "euphoria on demand" and he'll chase that sweet feeling for as long as he can. Give him a choice between the pain of reality or a bottle of euphoria and he'll choose the latter every time.

If you have a hard time believing this, notice what you do at a restaurant, for instance. If you start feeling the effects of your drink, you probably reach over and shove it away. You don't want to feel impaired, out of control or about to embarrass yourself. You don't compulsively search for a euphoriant to alter your mood. You use alcohol only in the context of food, a religious or social occasion; it's not a central feature of your life.

Solving problems with alcohol

Often you'll hear a friend or co-worker say things like, "Boy, the only way I cope with stress on the job is to wrap myself around a couple of drinks when I get home." Or, "With Bob and the kids away, a couple of drinks makes me feel less lonely." Or "Nothing makes me sleep like a drink or two." The problem is that for those with stress, loneliness or sleep disorders, alcohol — sneaky stuff that it is — will work for a while. But about the time a problem seems to be solved, the symptom of tolerance will show up and the drinking will start to *cause* stress, loneliness and insomnia. It's a paradox that alcohol will give your alcoholic more of everything he originally drank to avoid.

Preoccupation with alcohol

This symptom of alcoholism is fairly well understood by most, with TV showing us many examples of the agitated alcoholic in his office, nervously checking his wristwatch, waiting for 5 pm and drinking time. This is one form of preoccupation but by no means the only one. How about the homemaker who snaps at the kids to get to school so she can pour the day's first iced-tea tumbler full of wine? How about the man who wishes the wedding would finally end so that he could get to the champagne? How about the office manager who constantly worries whether she has enough wine or beer locked in her bedroom closet? This is referred to in recovery circles as "securing your supply." Buy four cases of distilled spirits and then worry whether five wouldn't be better.

Put a stopwatch on the average alcoholic and you'll find that he spends an inordinate amount of time securing his supply, drinking it and recovering from a hangover. No wonder he doesn't know what to do with all that spare time when he recovers!

Response to the first drink

Do you remember your first drink of alcohol? If you're a true social drinker, chances are good that you don't. Why would you? It did nothing for you with the possible exception of making you feel grown-up. If you do remember it, it probably had something to do with the social context at the time (religious ceremony, 21st birthday, etc.).

Pose that same question to your alcoholic and you'd better prepare yourself for a dramatic response: "Remember my first drink? Boy do I! My first drink was wonderful. It made me better looking, thinner, more charming and loquacious. I could dance better and for the first time in my life, I felt comfortable in my own skin." She might go on to say that she always felt as if she grew up with a hole in her personality — she didn't seem to fit in, to feel normal, to be a part of anything. That first drink, however, filled up that hole like a key in a well-oiled lock.

Is it any wonder why alcoholics try to fill that hole with liquor as long as they can? The fact that many alcoholics react to their first drink of alcohol in such a dramatic manner is inescapable.

Continuing to use after major problems

As a social drinker, chances are you'd drop that occasional drink in a hot minute if for some reason it gave you minor medical problems. Why not? It doesn't mean that much to you anyway; you do it mostly to be social.

Alcoholics, however, often encounter terrific problems with the way they drink. They get busted for driving while impaired, they go to jails, push their wives around, watch families disappear, lose jobs — and none of it will make them give up their alcohol. In fact, give any true alcoholic a choice between drinking and the things valued by most others and he'll take the drink.

Often, a woman comes to my office to talk about her boyfriend's or husband's alcoholism. She is positive that his drinking will stop if she only makes him choose between his alcohol and his "deep love for me." I would have to tell her not to be so sure. She often came back days later, crestfallen and in tears because her alcoholic made his choice.

When an alcoholic is young, those kinds of choices are easy: "Do you want to go to the school dance or drink beer?" But as we grow older, the choices become harder: "Do you want to keep that job or continue drinking?" Then come the truly hard ones: "Do you want your family or your booze?" And ultimately, "Do you want to live or drink?" Whether or not an alcoholic makes a conscious choice at any of these junctures, if he continues to drink, he's made the choice. Often I've asked an alcoholic, "Did you stop drinking when you ran into and killed those kids?" Almost always the answer is "no."

This symptom of "continued use" is most responsible for taking the alcoholic to the classic termination options found in Chapter 2 (*It's a Disease*): incarceration, psychiatric hospital or death. It's the intersection where logic and the reality of this disease collide. It doesn't make sense that a person would throw everything away for alcohol, but she will if she refuses recovery. This is by no means understandable. It's to be accepted and dealt with, not understood.

Why? I believe that alcoholics, as this book's epigraph from Goethe's *Faust* points out, confuse poison with medicine. To a recovering alcoholic, liquor is a poison. But the practicing alcoholic doesn't see it that way. To him or her, it's a *medicine*. Throw anything you can at them — stress, illness, death, unemployment, abandonment — and they'll think, "Well, with all this calamity, thank God I still have my medicine!" With treatment, they'll come to believe that alcohol is not a medicine but a toxin, and that they're killing themselves and their loved ones with it on the installment plan.

Chapter 6

Enabling

...to be restored, our sickness must grow worse.
T. S. Eliot, *Four Quartets*

One of the toughest tasks a therapist must perform has nothing to do with "wet" or even highly-resistant alcoholics. Those pale in comparison with having to explain to a woman who prides herself on a lifetime of service and compassion — or a man who may love his alcoholic more than anyone or anything else in the world — that their love and support may not be *helping* their alcoholic solve his or her drinking problem.

There is a word to describe how friends or family members help alcoholics stay in their disease — the word is "enabling." Look it up in the dictionary and you'll notice that it sounds so, well, *pleasant*: "To make feasible, or possible." So, if a parent offers money, transportation, another chance, a car, or a "get out of jail" card to an alcoholic, that's an attempt to make something possible, according to Webster. So what's the problem? The problem is that enabling provides a warm, moist climate for alcoholism. Most of my family clients over the years have had this type of dialogue with me:

Counselor: What have you been doing over the last few years to make your alcoholic stop drinking?

Parent: Well, I've given him money whenever he needed it; I've provided food and his old room upstairs; I've gotten him out of a jam in the middle of the night; I've given him our car; made excuses to his boss; cleaned his clothes for job interviews; got him a place to live and cleaned it...

Spouse: I withhold affection, sex and companionship; I don't pick up after him or clean his clothes.

Counselor: I hear lots of love and concern here. I also hear that one of you provides while the other withholds. Let me now ask, does it seems to work?

(Slight pause while they look around the room and remember that they're sitting with an alcoholism counselor).

Both: Not very well, we guess.

Counselor: You've been at this for several years haven't you? Can you foresee a time when these behaviors *might* work?

Both: We guess not.

Counselor: Might now be the time to take another tack and try something that has a better chance of succeeding?

What ultimately happens when you keep enabling? The same thing that happens to alcoholics who keep drinking — depression, frustration and anger. Keep doing it long enough and you'll become like the many other couples who, after many years of doing the drinking/enabling tango, enter my office for counseling. I'll introduce myself and make a mental note that they both look worn out, depressed and very sick. So sick, in fact, that I'll have to ask what may seem to be a very silly question: "Which one of you has the drinking problem?" Timidly, one of them will raise a hand. This one has spent the last few years awash with alcohol; the other has spent the last few years vainly trying to make the alcoholic quit — and the amazing thing is that both look so low they could parachute off a dime. So low, in fact, that I can't tell which is the alcoholic!

That's where enabling leads. And to add insult to injury, it doesn't even work. How do I know? Because I always ask the alcoholic — in front of the spouse or parent.

Counselor: Barbara, is there anything Jeff can do or not do, say or not say, threaten or cajole, cook or not cook, yell or whisper, provide or withhold that will have any effect on your decision to use alcohol?
Barbara: No.

I've asked this question a thousand times and the answer is always "no."

And it never fails to produce a surprised look on the face of the non-alcoholic. So why doesn't enabling work?

It's important to understand that between alcoholics and their enablers there exists an unspoken agreement. The alcoholic understands the agreement this way:

Provision A:
I (enabler's name here) hereby agree, in perpetuity, to provide said alcoholic with the following: beverage, food, lodging, cleaning service, bail bond money, clothes cleaning services, transportation (preferably a late model car), spending money and emergency road service on a 24-hour a day basis.

Provision B:
Said alcoholic promises to receive any and all services, make hundreds of vague promises and to drink unlimited amounts of alcohol.

Alcoholics become angry, severely agitated or frightened whenever this agreement collapses. And that's exactly what might have to happen for them to feel the consequences of their drinking. Alcoholics, when enabled, don't often learn what you want them to learn. Rather than experiencing and benefiting from their consequences, they often learn that if they mess up, they can always rattle their enabling system and either you or someone else will race to get them out of trouble.

Enablers, by doing for alcoholics what they should be doing for themselves, prolong their suffering and postpone everyone's entry into recovery. Thus we are led to distressing conclusion that if enablers are not part of the solution, they're part of the *problem*.

Enabling is an equal opportunity employer. Moms and Dads enable by failing to admit their "kid" is 44 and should have been on her own years ago. Spouses enable by cleaning up messes as fast as their alcoholic makes them. So efficient is the typical enabling system that many alcoholics who have fought the battle with the bottle for 20 years enter treatment and answer "no" to the question, "Do you understand the impact alcohol has had on your life?" They'll tell you that it's not really been a problem. They always have money, a car, an apartment with fresh sheets on the bed and good, nutritious food in their belly. They conveniently forget the fact that everything on that list is provided by enablers.

Remember the Jellinek or V-Chart from Chapter 2? Every alcoholic must make a Dante-like descent down the left side of the V-Chart. It's inevitable. In fact, it's the *process* each must go through before they get out of denial and say, "Hey, this stuff's ruining my life." It is suggested that alcoholics limit their time on the left side; the longer they spend there, the lower on the V-Chart they get and the worse off they become. Alcoholics, though, have different pain thresholds so the level from which they leave the left side for the right side (if they do) depends upon their pain tolerance. Enablers, through their loving but misguided actions, often prevent alcoholics from experiencing enough personal pain to motivate them into treatment. With the identification and collapse of this enabling system, the alcoholic gets on with the process of finding a personal threshold of pain.

No one likes to talk about allowing loved ones to feel pain. Talking about love seems more pleasant or more hopeful. Certainly, love has propelled many alcoholics to a better way of life — if the drinker hasn't been on the V-Chart very long. If alcoholism has been allowed to continue for too long a time, however — if the drinker is more than half-way down the V-Chart — the only thing that may motivate him into treatment is for you to stop the enabling (but not the love) and let him experience what he may need to experience.

You've already guessed, haven't you, that it's possible to plot *your* downward progression on a V-Chart? You started at a high level on the left side of the V when his drinking first became noticeable. You then became somewhat anxious but his excuses (as listed in Chapter 1) seemed reassuring. But as time went by, you noticed that your anxiety was getting worse. What if someone noticed? — his boss, for instance. What if he cracked up the car? Then things really got debilitating. You noticed yourself becoming more moody; that even the kids (even as young as two or three) were becoming affected. You started having headaches, neck spasms and sleepless nights. As you moved further down the V-Chart, you noticed you never did anything for yourself anymore. You looked 10 years older; you started getting fond of the idea of dying.

You've learned that for your alcoholic to recover, she must swing from the left side of V-Chart to recovery on the right side. *Your* own emergence from the chrysalis of the left side to the butterfly of the right will happen when you stop simply *reacting* to your alcoholic and start taking action yourself: owning your behaviors, owning your feelings, getting the help you need.

One actual call I took at NCADD/Phoenix was from a sweet but worried 80-year-old woman who couldn't understand why her boy was always drunk. She said she cooked and cleaned for him and gave him everything imaginable. When asked how old her boy was, she said "sixty." Forty years ago, perhaps, she and her "boy" entered into an unspoken but deadly contract that ruined both of their lives.

Recovery starts when the therapist takes the time to demonstrate to family members the extent of their enabling system and helps them permanently collapse it. Sanity begins when she demonstrates that just as alcoholics stop drinking when abstinence is less painful than drinking, enablers stop enabling when being part of the solution becomes less painful than being part of the problem.

Alcoholics always have enablers. They may be few; they may be many. But they're always around. In fact, if you know an alcoholic, all you must do is to look around for the enablers — good hearted people who are kind, loving and convinced that they can love someone into sobriety. I happen to believe that most organized religions can't deal with the reality of alcoholism. Such religions teach their practitioners to do good, to turn the other cheek, to help rather than hinder, to go the extra mile. This is wonderful stuff and I wish more people did it, but the problem begins when people of faith apply their good works to alcoholics — there, one can love thy neighbor to death.

So, it falls to the therapist the task of convincing enablers that something they've been doing for perhaps 50 years — perhaps the cornerstone of their lives; the very thing that gives meaning to their existence — won't work with alcoholics. Enablers so often must "learn to unlearn" what they know about interacting with their fellow human beings — especially one who has the disease of alcoholism.

Instructions as to how to collapse an alcoholic's enabling system through such tough love is never welcome at first (if at all). Some parents and spouses will listen to it as if the counselor is speaking Greek; others will mull it over and say, "We'll have to think about this for a while." Still others will tell you right up front that they've heard the enabling lecture before and they don't want to hear it again. (This may be more about the enabler's own abandonment issues.)

What they often hear is the counselor telling them to abandon their suffering alcoholic. They'll says things like "Well I can't just turn her out into the snow, can I?" "I can't throw him out without a roof over his head." "I can't just abandon my own daughter can I?"

If you're always imagining that it's snowing outside, I have this suggestion:

Simply get your alcoholic an apartment — for a month. Install him in it and tell him that the free ride at home has ended and that he has a month to find work. Work may be found at a car wash, sacking groceries or at a local fast food restaurant. At the end of the month, he'll get a paycheck. He may choose to spend all of this money on alcohol. However, if he chooses to give a portion of that paycheck to the apartment manager, he may live there another month; plus, with the leftover money he'll get to eat. If he chooses to do nothing during the month, he must find somewhere else to live and the means to eat. This is a choice, it's a tough choice but it's his choice and it's crystal clear.

Toward the end of the month, your alcoholic may come up with some excuse as to (1) why he couldn't find a job; or (2) what happened to the money. He'll beg you to take him back but that's not part of the original agreement. It will hurt him to "be tossed out in the snow" but at least you'll understand that his reaquaintance with the cold, fluffy stuff was his decision and his decision alone. You've not thrown him out; he's thrown himself out.

This is love — but it's tough. Very few parents can emotionally detach from an adult child, especially when that adult child is an alcoholic. That's why few stop their enabling behaviors — it goes against the grain of not only their religious belief but, seemingly, against the idea of marriage or parenthood itself.

This is why tough love should never be done alone. If you come to the conclusion that it's time for tough love, you'll be more likely to succeed if you become part of a larger system such as Al-Anon Family Groups. There, you'll encounter other parents and spouses who have similar stories. They've already been down this road — they've tried enabling and found it didn't work. Now they realize they're getting somewhere. They're part of a community. Telephone numbers are exchanged to provide needed support when yet another call comes from a crying alcoholic who says, "Dad, I screwed up again. I want to come home." Put in a call to one of your Al-Anon friends and he won't tell you what to do. However, he will ask these questions: "Hasn't that option been tried before? What makes you think it will work this time?"

Learning to defocus or detach from a practicing alcoholic is wonderful. But detaching without working on yourself in a Twelve-Step program is half a loaf. Practicing an Al-Anon program doesn't mean that your tough love will work. There are still a lot of "ifs." But I do know without a doubt what won't work — and that's to continue enabling.

Such a support group is not for the alcoholic; it's for you, the enabler. In fact, I submit that stopping enabling behaviors has less to do with your alcoholic and more to do with preserving your happiness and your sanity. Many's the time that a distraught family member has left my office convinced at last that she's going to start worrying about herself for a change. That she's going to do some of the things she's had to discontinue in order to focus obsessively on the alcoholic — she's going to exercise again; start doing things with girlfriends; start going to movies; start eating the right foods; start working out; start living. When this happens, the counseling session has been successful — a moral victory has been achieved — a giant leap has been taken. About every two days, I ask a tired, emotionally distressed woman, "So who's taking care of you?" This question is never answered verbally — her tears do all the talking.

One way of presenting the concept of tough love always seems to get through. You're probably aware that there's more than one type of love. There's the Valentine's Day type of love where candy and flowers are given. At the early stages of alcoholism, this type of love may help your alcoholic find something that works soon enough to make a difference. For the later stages of alcoholism, when most attempts to help have been exhausted, an even higher type of love can be called into play — in fact, it's the highest type of love you'll ever show to another. It's the ability to say, "I love you so much I'm willing to allow you to experience your consequences." Very few people can do this. Candy and flowers are much simpler. But removing yourself as a hindrance to the alcoholic's process allows him to start experiencing pain and, God willing, to join the millions of people who are recovering.

Chapter 7

Formally Intervening

The very last thing the alcoholic will ever want to see is all these people he's fed stories to sitting around talking to each other. If they do, their enabling will stop, the money will dry up and the game is over. And that's exactly what happens during a formal intervention.

We saw in the last chapter how identifying and collapsing enabling systems of alcoholics allows them (perhaps for the first time) to experience the consequences of their drinking. Awareness of such consequences, and the pain they produce, is *mandatory* in order for them to get well. They won't feel pain as long as enablers run interference for them. Identify and remove the enablers and the alcoholics' painful consequences will surface and worsen until they choose to make permanent changes in their lives.

Al-Anon Family Groups are rife with stories about spouses who practice tough love. One story is about the woman who made nightly trips outside to walk her drunk husband into the house where she would remove his clothing, put him in clean pajamas and somehow get him upstairs to bed. Then she would go back outside and move his car from the lawn and pull it properly into the garage. This was done night after night and every morning her husband would wake up in bed with no memory of what happened the night before.

Noticing that she seemed to be getting nowhere, she explored Al-Anon Family Groups. She came to understand that she was not helping her husband with this type of enabling behavior — she was hindering him. So, the next time it happened, she tried a new tack. When she heard the car go up on the lawn, she went outside and true to form, found her husband passed out behind the wheel. She attended to his comfort, loosened his clothing and laid him down on the front seat. Then she rolled down the windows a little for air, locked the doors, went into the house and went to sleep. Or at least *tried* to sleep because she knew she just took a huge risk — she just let the world in on some dirty little family secrets.

The next morning, her husband woke up — but not in a bed with clean sheets. He was in his car which was resting rather unceremoniously in the family rose bushes. Worse, there were neighbors around — looking into his car window, tending their yards. One doesn't suppose that this was enough to move him into treatment, but it did leave a lasting impression on him that his drinking had consequences.

Or how about the husband who gets a late night phone call from his wife pleading with him to bail her out of jail. Mindful of his support group training, and all the previous times he listened to her promises, the husband tells his wife

he loves her and leaves her in jail to meditate on the consequences of her drinking.

Many parents and spouses of an alcoholic have told a
counselor, "Yes, we stood strong together years ago but we
weakened." Putting up a united front against unacceptable
drinking behavior is good. Making sure that front stays
united is best.

Which brings us to the subject of the formal intervention.

Most people know about certain types of interventions
that are far less than formal. They know about getting in the
alcoholic's face; about getting together and going over to
"talk some sense into him." They know that hunting buddies
or co-workers sometimes "gang up" on an alcoholic and tell
him, "For God's sake Al, you gotta quit killin' yourself."

What they may not know is that these "confrontations,"
as they're called, don't work for at least four reasons. First,
these well-meaning happenings are never planned or rehearsed. Second, the family or friends never give any
thought to what the alcoholic needs to do to get help. If the
alcoholic says, "Okay, where do you want me to go?" a pre-
cious window of opportunity is lost as the startled family
starts thumbing through the phone book at 11 pm. Third,
confrontations don't work because the family and friends
state their case in a manner which insults or places the confrontation target on the defensive. And fourth, confrontations fail because the family is not ready to *permanently* collapse their enabling system.

"Confronters" make their way to the "confrontee's"
house in a disorganized fashion, blast their way past the
front door, insult the alcoholic with their ill-thought-out
pleas for moderation or abstinence, offer no advice about
getting help and lastly, allow the alcoholic (who has more
experience at this game than they do) to divide and conquer
them. Barely avoiding a fist fight, the concerned group

leaves the house with the uneasy feeling that they just made things worse.

So detrimental are such confrontations that it was always my practice to suggest to family members that they not be done.

Concerned family member: We've all just flown into Phoenix; we're only going to be together for two days but we want to confront our mother while we're here — any tips?
The Author: Yes, enjoy the sunshine, play a little golf and fly back home.

The type of confrontation I hear this person planning will probably be so destructive that I suggest, unless their alcoholic is having a medical emergency, they return at a later date for a discussion of the formal intervention process and referral to an experienced, trained interventionist. But if they're simply going to race in on her, get in her face, drag up a host of nebulous, undocumented charges, tell her that she's always been a terrible disappointment and then leave town — that's abusive and frankly I don't want to be a part of it.

There are those who say that any type of confrontation is better than none at all — I don't agree. I believe that a poorly-done confrontation poses a threat not only to the alcoholic but to members of the concerned family. Confronting an intoxicated, paranoid alcoholic who might have a loaded pistol hidden in his armchair is a highly dangerous activity.

A much more systematic, methodical and proven way of challenging denial and getting help for your alcoholic is the formal intervention. Designed to replace the confrontation, the formal intervention is the brainchild of many therapists who noticed confrontations weren't working and developed a procedure that would. It is a positive process designed to defeat a negative process (alcoholism) and has proved to be such a valuable instrument for change that thousands of alcoholics owe it their lives.

It is generally accepted that it takes a crisis to get the attention of an alcoholic. The intervention process works because it doesn't wait for a crisis to come to the alcoholic (that could be harmful to himself or others). It creates a "therapeutic" crisis and takes it to him. It's inhumane to allow an alcoholic to plunge down the left side of the Jellinek Chart without being allowed to experience such a "controlled" crisis. An intervention also clarifies choices. Once he's presented with a chance to recover, his support system comes to understand that if he takes that first drink again, it's because he wants to.

The process also works because it's so well thought out that nothing's left to chance. Every excuse is anticipated, every step is practiced, every word is carefully considered. Formal intervention teams not only kill the alcoholic's enabling system but, by refusing to allow it to resurrect, drive a stake through its heart.

The best way to start learning about formal interventions is to visit a library or recovery-type bookstore and ask for books or video tapes on interventions. (See the suggested readings at the back of the book for some suggestions.) Videos which effectively dramatize a formal intervention are also available at certain NCADD affiliates. Larger hospitals and treatment centers often have a trained interventionist on staff who does public information sessions and interventions as part of their marketing effort.

Prior to embarking on the intervention process, it's best to know whether the target of concern has medical insurance (public or private) or access to an employee assistance program (EAP). Many larger, progressive companies have EAPs affiliated with their Human Resources office, although so-called corporate downsizing has resulted in a false economy whereby many wonderful EAPs have been eliminated.

There are three questions that need to be asked of your health insurance carrier (and there's no need to break anyone's anonymity to ask them). The first is "Does the current policy provide coverage for chemical dependency treatment?" Don't be too surprised if the answer is "no." Those shopping for health plans rarely inquire about such benefits until it's too late. If the answer is "yes," the second question becomes "How much does it cover?" This will be explained in terms of either dollars ("Up to $8,000," for instance) or days ("Two days of detox; three days of treatment," etc.). The third and last question is "Do you have a list of preferred providers?" In other words, has the policy underwriter already made formal financial arrangements with local alcoholism clinics, hospitals, treatment centers or health maintenance organizations (HMOs)? If so, that's where you start. It makes no sense to thrash around looking for a formal interventionist if your health plan already has a preferred provider of alcoholism services with an experienced interventionist on the payroll.

If there is no insurance coverage or if the policy has coverage but no preferred providers, it becomes the task of the concerned family to search for and hire the services of an independent interventionist — i.e., one who doesn't have a financial relationship or affiliation with a treatment center, hospital or HMO. Working with an NCADD affiliate to find such a person will prove helpful.

The name "interventionist" is somewhat of a misnomer as it implies that he or she will actually intervene on the target of concern. Not true. The interventionist will steer the intervention process and do what needs to be done, but it's the target's enabling system that does the intervening. In fact, so well rehearsed will the intervention team become that when the target is finally present, the interventionist has only to act as a peacekeeper.

When an interventionist is found, the first thing he or she will do is determine if there seems to be enough of a problem to merit an intervention. Of course, people don't usually walk in off the street to engage a total stranger in the subject of a loved one's drinking problem. But on rare occasions, a religious family or church community with a strong taboo against alcohol will dislike the social drinking of a member. This is not an alcoholism problem — this is a matter of church doctrine and the interventionist will not want to get involved.

He or she will also be on guard against the family having a conflict of interest (divorce or child custody case, etc.) and a desire to "set up" the target. The interventionist will also look for mental illness and will pick up on it if he hears a discussion of mental health agencies already working with the target. Lastly, the assessment will yield important information regarding the potential target's health (heart condition, HIV diagnosis, etc.)

Don't be surprised if, during the assessment, the interventionist is more interested in facts than feelings. The last thing he wants is for a family member's anger to open up. He will also avoid using the word "alcoholic" at this time. Such words may be understood by the family to mean a derelict rather than a valuable family member who has a disease he didn't ask for. Better to use a more generally understood, less stigmatizing word such as "problem."

If this assessment provides the interventionist with a true picture of a drinking problem, he will help you assemble a team of persons with enough influence over the alcoholic's life as to provide him with no realistic choice other than to get help. In the absence of the actual target, however, the interventionist would violate ethical guidelines if he were to make a clinical diagnosis of alcoholism.

Everyone influences another. Bosses and supervisors influence. The police force has influence; families provide love, nurturing and financial support — that's influence. What a formal intervention does is harness that influence for good. It inventories those with influence over the alcoholic, assembles them and if the person of concern decides to permanently do something about his alcoholism, that love, nurturing and financial support will continue to be offered. If the target doesn't want to play, however, the influence and/or loving support will either be totally withdrawn or severely curtailed.

When concerned families first hear about the role influence plays when assembling an intervention team, they're usually at a loss for names. They will think first of parents and perhaps a spouse, then the trail gets cold. But what about the employer or co-workers? Don't they represent influence? Often, a concerned family member — who 30 minutes ago said she wanted to do something because "he's killing himself" — will suddenly turn timid at the thought of involving a human resources department, boss or supervisor. "Won't that get him fired?" she'll ask. The interventionist may then ask, "If you do nothing, won't his drinking get him dead?"

Children and grandchildren, too, represent influence — the influence of available love. Grandchildren are often the forgotten element of interventions. Many of those over retirement age won't get sober for themselves: "Who cares? I'm getting older and I'm retired" is the way they'll put it. But let it be known to alcoholic grandparents that their grandchildren are suddenly going to become withheld and they'll fall all over themselves getting into treatment. Small children who for some reason don't wish to verbalize may choose to draw a picture or write a letter.

Others who come to mind when influence is mentioned are siblings, members of the clergy, fishing buddies, former college roommates or church/club members. If a team member cannot be physically present during the intervention, she may want to use a conference call hookup or provide a video tape.

As mentioned in Chapter 6 on *Enabling*, intervening works best when the target of concern is still fairly high on the left side of the Jellinek Chart. The lower she goes, the more connections to family and friends that are lost and the harder it is to intervene. The formal intervention process is so good, however, that it can work even when the target of concern is in late stages of alcoholism — when very few supportive people exist.

Interventionist: Who has influence in this person's life? Who gives this person money, buys him alcohol, supports him in his disease?

Client: Well, he has no friends or relatives left. But he does get welfare checks, supplemental security income (SSI) and food stamps, although I don't suppose that human services agencies like the idea of him drinking up public assistance dollars.

Assemble a few office workers from those agencies and you'll have the makings of a pretty good intervention.

There are three types who don't belong in a formal intervention. One is the person who can't control her anger. Many team members will, of course, be somewhat angry at the target of concern. But a person whose anger is so out of control that they can't sit in the same room with a target without starting a fight has no business there. Your interventionist, as he helps develop the team, will be on guard for this individual and know how to deal with her.

Another is the target's drinking buddy who may be an alcoholic but sees no reason to stop his own drinking. In the early days of interventions, the target's drinking companion was never even considered as a team member. That has softened somewhat over the years and today, he may be appropriate if he has already taken steps toward his own recovery. Thus, if the target says, "Well what about you, Bill? You drink as much as I do," the team member will be able to honestly say, "Yes, that's right, I used to do that. But I'm starting to see the negative effect it's having on my life — and I want to stop." When a drinking companion says this — or at least intimates that he may not be a fellow imbiber anymore — his contribution to the intervention is significant.

How would an interventionist know if someone being considered as a team member has an untreated drinking problem? By suggesting that each member — for the duration of the intervention — maintain a program of abstinence. Each time the team returns to meet with the interventionist the question will be asked: "How did we do with our abstinence?" Those who originally agreed to refrain from alcohol but find they cannot will soon make themselves known.

The final person who doesn't belong on the team is someone who is a victim of the target's domestic violence. It's better for her to remain on the sidelines lest she become the sole recipient of her alcoholic's anger.

Once formation of the team is complete, their first task is to get acquainted and discuss the target's alcohol problem. This is done to level the playing field regarding the severity of the drinking problem. Some relatives or friends may live out of town or out of state and not have first-hand knowledge of how much his disease has progressed. They'll have to be told this by other team members.

Another reason is because alcoholics — due to the insidious nature of their disease — have plenty of time to develop "divide and conquer" tactics with families, friends and supervisors. In other words, alcoholics learn that it's in their best interest to share with their support system only a little of what's really going on in their life and then pray that the system never gets together and talks. Their supervisor is told, "How can you say I have a problem at work, when it's not a problem at home?" They'll say the same thing to the spouse and claim their boss is okay with it. Such a feat of skill is reminiscent of the performer who exhausted himself on the Ed Sullivan Show while trying to keep a number of plates spinning on tall poles. Again, the very last thing the alcoholic will ever want to see is all these people he's fed stories to sitting around talking to each other. In fact, he'll admonish them not to. If they do, the enabling will stop, the money will dry up, the plates will crash to the floor and the game will be over. And that's exactly what happens during a formal intervention.

When all the alcoholic's stories and alibis are exploded, when it is finally clear to all team members that a major drinking problem is at hand, the interventionist will likely take that opportunity to introduce the team to their second activity — their "homework." The homework is nothing more than the team's scripted and edited approach to saying what needs to be said to the target of concern. In an old-style confrontation, no one knew what they were going to say but chances are great that it was delivered as a "*you*-statement." You-statements are generally abusive, accusatory and guaranteed to put the alcoholic on the defensive. A typical you-statement goes, "You're a failure and you're always going to be a failure."

Who wants to hear someone call them a failure? That's no way to get someone in treatment. Further, the you-statement is not very loving; it does a very poor job of describing facts you know first-hand; it doesn't explain how you feel; it is not affirming by any stretch and offers the alcoholic no options toward getting help.

Formal interventions, however, use "I-statements" which anyone can learn and practice by taking assertiveness training classes. A well-crafted, non-judgmental series of I-statements provide the ill person with a pledge of love. They will describe an actual incident which occurred when the target of concern was under the control of alcohol. They will tell the target exactly how you felt about it. They will affirm that he's a good person (husband, father, friend) who normally doesn't act that way. And finally, they'll tell him exactly what you want him to do. Here's what a series of well-crafted I-statements sounds like during an intervention:

1. Mark, I love you very much; you're the father of my children and I want most of all to continue our life together.
2. Two weeks ago, you come home from a bar and I watched as you knocked down the back of our garage with your truck.
3. I felt very frightened when I saw this.
4. I know that when you're sober something like that would never happen.
5. I'm more and more convinced that you have a drinking problem. I'm getting (help, support, counseling) and I'd like you to join me in recovery.

Notice how these I-statements are not accusatory. Mark hears a statement of love; he is told about what you actually saw; he knows how you felt about it; he was affirmed that he's a good guy and comes to know that you'd like to see him get help. It was more about you than it was about him. (The beauty of I-statements is that they weren't designed simply for those who are alcoholic. They were designed to facilitate good communication between human beings — between couples, between management and labor, between parent and child).

Each intervention team member is asked to come up with a few ideas that with help from the interventionist will be crafted into carefully-worded I-statements. Later, these statements will be rehearsed and read to the target of concern. That's right, they'll be read right off a script. The formal intervention, when you're face to face with the target, is no time for thinking. All the thinking is done by the team prior to the appearance of the target.

Once the I-statements are edited, it's time for task number three: deciding where the target should go for help. Help may come in the form of attendance at a prescribed number of support group meetings; at a detox; inpatient or outpatient care; a series of educational sessions on drinking sponsored by the target's employer. In all cases, help is the object and the team must decide how to get it. It won't be the end of the world if two treatment or support group choices are presented to the target. That may allow her a certain amount of control over her destiny and/or allow her to save face.

Commendable to the intervention process is the team's careful research on exactly which treatment center (if any) the target will enter and the route he'll take to get there. Nothing's left to chance. After the first round of I-statements is over, the interventionist will ask the target whether he's amenable to doing what the team suggests — that he get help. By this time, the powerful I-statements have produced their intended effect and the alcoholic is listening for once rather than doing all the talking. With all the heavy artillery in the room, agreeing to get help is his only real option. In other words, he's being asked whether he wants to continue drinking or to admit a problem and take steps to correct it. If he says "yes," he keeps this warm, supportive group around him. If he says "no," he'll have to start replacing them with weird people whose gene pool is in obvious need of a filter.

After the target says "yes" (and they do most of the time), he'll probably start some verbal tap dancing. He'll amend that "yes" statement to say, "Gosh, I'm awfully busy at work and soon as the Figby contract is finished, I'm good for it." This excuse has already been anticipated by the team and the target soon remembers that his supervisor and members of the human resources department are within 20 feet of him. A second amendment is then introduced to supplant the first one: "I'll need to go home first and pack." This dodge, too, is foreseen and someone on the team will say, "No, you're already packed." True to form, just out of the target's line of sight is a small suitcase full of everything he'll need to get through the first few days at a detox or treatment center.

Even if the target is a freak for efficiency, sees the intervention and says, "Okay, let's go," he still needs to sit down and listen to those who have something loving but firm to say to him. It may also be a good idea for everyone to sign a pre-written contract after the "yes" is heard.

Let's assume for the moment that our target is reluctant to get help. That's where activity four comes in. From somewhere in the intervention room, a "consequences list" is produced. This is a pre-written list that details the tough measures the team will do (*will do*, not just *think* about doing) if the target is reluctant. Upon hearing a "no," the interventionist will say that the team appreciates the candor of the target and now hopes the target will appreciate the candor of the team. (The target probably should take a deep breath at this point because she won't like what she's going to hear.) The team is going to spell out exactly how they plan to collapse her enabling system; they'll let her know, perhaps, about the divorce, the ensuing child custody battle and about picking up that final paycheck. She'll be told about the locks on the house and how she'll need photographs of the children or grandchildren to remind her of how they look because chances are she won't be seeing them very often.

Tough? Sure it is. But you don't do formal interventions to make people like you. You do them to save someone's life. If the target fails to recover, she may die. But because of this marvelous process, the family and friends may truthfully say, "Back on such-and-such a date, we tried something and we did the very best we could."

From my experience with the formal intervention process, I offer these observations:

1. Clients always ask, "How will I know if the intervention is going to be a success?" I've learned to tell them that if the intervention is done correctly, if the right team is chosen, if the team really hangs together and gets into recovery through Al-Anon, if everyone on the team knows what's going on with the alcoholic and steps have been taken to identify and collapse her enabling system, then the intervention is already a success before the target of concern ever walks into the room!

2. Wives and lovers usually ask, "But if I stop enabling him, won't he simply look for another enabler?" Yes, I say as gingerly as I can, he may. He might find that wonderful gal who agrees that his drinking is not a problem but a terrible misunderstanding. He might be tempted to go down this road (and the spouse will learn to deal with it in her recovery group). But even though an alcoholic may seek out other enablers, subsequent periods of enabling always gets shorter and shorter. (No one enables like family!) That special gal who "understands" will quickly get perturbed when she discovers that her newly-found drinking companion is big on "gimme" and small on income production.

3. Clients ask, "Yes, but what if she walks out of the intervention?" Once more, when the intervention is done correctly, when the enabling system is collapsed and team members are in their own support groups, the intervention is already a success. The target of concern is invited to attend the intervention and listen; she is welcome to

stay or she may wish to walk out. In any case, it's a done deal before she gets there. At times, when I am explaining an intervention to an anxious family, I will, without warning, walk out of the counseling room. After about five minutes, I reappear before the puzzled family and say, "See, that's the worst thing that can happen."

4. Families and friends in agreement as to the danger of a person's alcoholism may disagree as to the risk of formally intervening. Therapists who routinely explain interventions often notice that while a spouse might be enthusiastic about the idea, one of her adult children might persistently ask, "But won't Dad be mad?" Her reluctance, perhaps caused by her regression to the traumatic years when her drunken father terrorized the family, may be such that the intervention is scuttled. Education, it seems, is being provided but group healing has not yet taken place nor has group consensus been reached. I believe it may behoove NCADD counseling staffs and other community-based providers to offer the same kind of mediation to families of alcoholics facing possible *end-of-relationship* decisions that hospices provide to families facing *end-of-life* decisions.

5. An astute team member will sometimes catch the true irony of the formal intervention process. Ostensibly, the alcoholic is the target; in reality, however, it's the alcoholic's enabling system that is intervened upon. When that happens, the alcoholic only has two options and one of them is horrible.

6. The answer to the question, "Can't the target simply go through the motions of getting help and then go back to his old behavior when the heat is off?" is "Not easily." This can be done with a confrontation but as we've seen,

an intervention is a horse of a different color. If the team notices that there is slippage in the target's original desire to get help, they may wish to reassemble the original intervention team and read (or re-read) to him their list of consequences.

7. It's not unusual for a former intervention target to graduate from inpatient or outpatient treatment, work a good AA program and still have unresolved issues of mistrust and anger stemming from the intervention itself. Unless he's told that it's okay to have and to deal with these issues, he might continually ask himself, "Why am I able to enjoy recovery so much and still be angry at my family because of the intervention?"

My article "Healing the Intervention" (March/April, 1991 issue of *Professional Counselor* Magazine) provides a framework for dealing with issues raised by formal interventions. Under normal circumstances, it involves little more than reassembling the original intervention team (with the interventionist) and allowing the former target to express feelings of residual anger, embarrassment or general discomfort — and certainly *gratitude* — stemming from the team's earlier expression of tough love. In other words, this time the target speaks and the team listens. For this kind of healing to happen, however, your interventionist must clearly understand that even though they save lives, interventions are powerful enough to create their own issues; that it would be unethical for them to pretend that these issues don't exist; and that clinicians cannot be expected to treat these issues if they're unaware that their patient began his recovery in an intervention.

Chapter 8

Powerlessness

God grant me the serenity to accept the things I cannot change, courage to change the things I can, and wisdom to know the difference.
                                    The Serenity Prayer

This chapter discusses one of the concepts you will encounter when you start getting the help you deserve. That's right, the help *you* deserve. Surprised? Offended? Many are when they seek treatment for a loved one and hear the therapist say, "Let's start with what's going on with you." It usually sounds like this:

You: But you don't understand. *He's* the alcoholic.
Counselor: I do understand. But right now, don't you deserve to be in good emotional shape to make the decisions you may soon have to make?

You: There's nothing wrong with me that his getting sober can't fix.

Counselor: Tell me, what do you do for fun?

You: I like to play cards, have people over for dinner, go to movies, work out, eat lunch with girlfriends, take walks in the morning, that kind of stuff.

Counselor: Sounds wonderful. When's the last time you did any of that?

You: (After thinking long and hard for a few moments) *Five years ago.*

Your therapist is not at all surprised at this statement. She's had a hunch that (1) you didn't sign up for this alcoholism-in-the-family stuff; (2) your guy's drinking has had a powerful effect on you and the children; (3) you've spent so much time worrying about him that you've neglected yourself; (4) you take care of everyone in the family and no one takes care of you; (5) if you don't stop you may become just as sick as he is.

She also has a hunch that having friends over is a risky business because you never know which husband is going to walk through the door. Will it be the drunk husband, the cruel husband, the nice husband or the rageaholic who soon makes the furniture start flying? Or perhaps it's the husband who is calmly reading the paper or passed out in the nude?

If you're really tired of living like this and want to get help for yourself, get it now. Don't just react to *him*. Don't wait for that glorious sunny day when the heavens open and he finally decides to recover. That day may never come. And if you do desire to get help, there's no better place to get it than Al-Anon Family Groups.

Al-Anon is where you go from the left to the right side of the Jellinek Chart. That's where the recovery is. While attending such groups, you'll discover whole rooms full of people just like you. You can laugh with them, cry with them, exchange phone numbers, share your family secrets with them and they'll understand — they've said and done almost exactly the same things. And best of all, you'll discover that you're not alone; that they, too, have tried in vain to make an alcoholic quit drinking. They realize it can't be done; and they stay in Al-Anon because they don't want to forget it and start getting crazy again.

It's not unique to find a friend in Al-Anon who keeps attending even though she and her alcoholic are no longer together. If you ask her why, she'll probably tell you an embarrassing personal story about marrying alcoholics. She may describe this not-so-rare phenomenon by saying: "I don't know what it is, but it's like I have antenna on my forehead that can pick out a needy drinker even in a room with 100 other guys." She knows that if she doesn't get a weekly dose of Al-Anon reality about her preference for exciting, off-the-wall men who happen to be alcoholic, she knows she has a good chance of marrying yet another one.

Likewise, it's common to find a friend in Al-Anon whose alcoholic sobered up long ago. So, you may ask him, why do you continue to go? He'll probably tell you that he originally got Al-Anon support because the woman he loves drank alcoholically. But he still needs support because now that she's stopped, the thought of her starting again makes him crazy.

There's a word they use in Al-Anon that best describes all this. The word is "powerless." No one ever likes to think of themselves as powerless. It goes against the grain of human nature. Nevertheless, it's a great word and your recovery will depend on how well you embrace it. But "powerless" doesn't mean "helpless," "hopeless" or even "clueless." By the term powerless, I mean getting out from under a delusion — a delusion that you've got everything under good control. Attending Al-Anon and announcing that you've got everything under control is rather like your alcoholic attending an AA meeting and announcing that booze has always been kind to him. No, the word powerless means that you are not — nor have you ever been — nor will you ever be — in control of an alcoholic. That's among the many things (as the Serenity Prayer says) you "cannot change." Al-Anon celebrates the things you do have power over ("things you can change") — your feelings, your behaviors and your choices. This is the power to re-take control of your life.

So how do you know what you can change and what you can't? You've got to go outside of yourself to find that answer: "(grant me) wisdom to know the difference." Is it any wonder why every Al-Anon (and AA) meeting either opens or closes with the Serenity Prayer?

Interestingly enough, the word "powerless" is also discussed at length at Alcoholics Anonymous. Rather than admit powerlessness over alcohol, alcoholics will distort reality by developing a long list of alibis which they will embrace until their downward slide on the Jellinek Chart becomes so painful that their alibi system collapses. To avoid taking any therapeutic action, they make promises or resolutions by the score; they blame their problem on their geographical circumstances and move from town to town or state to state; rather than taking ownership of their addiction, they blame it on others; they attempt to assuage guilt by spending extravagant sums of money on Christmas and birthday presents; rather than admit how much they drink, they hide their alcohol use; they avoid face-to-face contact with people in favor of midnight telephone calls where they cry and say the same things over and over; they shun peers and non-alcoholics in favor of inferiors who make them feel less guilty; they gamble to get instant financial relief; and lastly, they avoid the responsibilities of family life in favor of that citadel of alcoholic normalcy called the "bar."

After reviewing this kind of life, your alcoholic may come to the conclusion that she always failed to exhibit control over alcohol or any other mood-altering chemical. And once that control is gone, she'll never get it back. As a member of Al-Anon, you may also benefit from examining your life and, like your alcoholic, come to the conclusion that you, too, failed to exhibit control over her drinking. Power, and the evil twins *force* and *control*, is an illusion. You and your alcoholic might be hanging on to that illusion to the point of insanity.

The words "power" and "control" suggest strongly that someone must act a certain way after your power or control is exerted. "When I demand this from him, this is what he will do." "When I threaten to leave her because of her drinking, that will force her to stop." Fat chance. Not only will he not do what you want but he'll be angry at you for trying to control him. What I suggest is that you drop the word *power* and pick up the word *influence*. This word will get you somewhere as it correctly infers that while you may try to show your alcoholic a better way, he's free to make his own choices (just like you are) and he will ultimately do what he wants.

Notice in Chapter 7 on *Formally Intervening* that I used the word *influence* rather than the word *power* when discussing the development of the intervention team. I also noted that "you-statements" don't work because they are accusatory and smack of an attempt to control. Employ the kinder and gentler "I-statements" in your intervention, however, and don't be surprised if you and your team *influence* your alcoholic into treatment. However, no one on the team has the *power* to make an alcoholic stop drinking.

Parents understand this — or should. They influence all the time but woe to the parents of a teenager who believes they can rule through power. The teenager will soon show them otherwise. The alcoholism therapist may influence someone to review his drinking history and conclude that it's always been an exercise in powerlessness. The therapist knows that through the formal intervention process, the alcoholic is left with no other realistic option but treatment. But the wise therapist understands — and doesn't take it personally — that the alcoholic will ultimately do what she wants.

So it seems that whether we like it or not, we are powerless. We may and should use our influence for the good of others. But we must never forget that we have no true power over them. Otherwise, we set ourselves up for failure.

Surprisingly, world powers are essentially powerless — it just takes longer for them to realize it. Shortly after World War I, the victorious Allied Powers, forgetting how Christians and Muslims historically interacted, cobbled together a loose confederation of Balkan states and invented Yugoslavia. With the collapse of Communism in the late 1980s, Yugoslavia blew up with a loud and bloody bang. Likewise, from the 1940s to the 1970s, France and the United States thought they could have their way with Indochina; in 1981 it was the Soviet Union and Afghanistan; and in 1994, Russia and Chechnya.

An understanding of powerlessness is good medicine for you and your alcoholic. One of the reasons why he should be steered to a methodical, habitual program of recovery is because it will provide him with a vehicle for remembering his last drunk. When he shares at a support group or talks one-on-one with another alcoholic, he will be reminded that he tried to successfully drink alcohol and couldn't. Now that he's aware of his powerlessness, he works a methodical program of recovery to ensure that he doesn't forget. Concurrently, you ensure that you don't forget the last time you tried to control his drinking and failed.

Chapter 9

Recovery

When he gets into recovery, he'll learn that sobriety is a horse that bucks; staying on it means changing almost every aspect of his life.

Look up the word "recovery" in the dictionary and you'll find it means "being restored to a normal state." Can your alcoholic restore herself to normalcy simply by not drinking? In treatment circles, this is called being "dry." Putting down the bottle is a wonderful start but what about changing her attitude? What about being less critical and less negative? What about learning how to deal with life on life's terms? How about losing all that anger she seems to have stored up over the years? Accomplish that and she will accomplish true recovery. Nothing less will do.

If you're buying and reading books on alcoholism, you and your alcoholic have probably had this kind of dialogue:

Alcoholic: You told me months ago that you wanted out of the marriage; that you were tired of always coming in second to my drinking. Well, guess what? I haven't had a drink now for the last three months and I feel great! So what do you say? Let's call up that divorce lawyer and tell him it was all a big mistake.

You: I still want you out of my life.

Alcoholic: Maybe you didn't hear me right. I haven't had a drink in a long time. If alcohol was the problem with our marriage, then the problem's over — finished — kaput.

You: Not so fast. I've watched you stay dry for three months now and you've been miserable. In fact, you've become just one more alcoholic who wants to drink and, frankly, the world does not need another one of those. You haven't changed a bit. You're still obnoxious, self-centered, rude, lazy, negative, whining and you've taken the art of self-pity to new heights. Maybe you are not drinking but I still want no part of you.

As often as this dialogue occurs, it's surprising that it's never been dignified with a formal name — so let's just refer to it as Huge Insight No. 1: "Drunk or dry, you're still a pain." This is when the alcoholic learns for the first time that there's more to recovery than just not drinking. This is disappointing. Would that he could continue to equate sobriety with a grandiose display of temporary abstinence as he could then continue to feed you all the promises you can hold. When he gets into recovery he'll learn that sobriety is a horse that bucks; staying on it means changing almost every aspect of his life.

There are those who will often discount recovery by saying that so-and-so hasn't had a drink in years. That may be true, but the critical questions are, "Is that person happy? Is she delighted with her sobriety or does she really wish she were drinking again? Does he truly enjoy his abstinence or does he just surround himself with enough distractions and busy-work to keep the plug in the jug? Would you like to have what that person seems to have?"

If recovery is not just abstinence then what else is it not? Well, recovery is not just an attempt by your alcoholic to "play along with your silly little game." And it certainly is not an emotional upheaval that disappears after the revival tent is struck. Recovery is serious; it's not to be undertaken lightly nor is it a game.

Neither is it a disease that must be struggled against — as if alcoholism were part of some glorious workers' revolution. This may explain why those who remain on the outside of support groups seldom, in my opinion, make progress. They believe that alcoholism must be fought and thus their lives are constantly on a war footing.

To the contrary — alcoholism must be surrendered to and dealt with, not fought. As one who grew up soon after World War II, the author well remembers that the word *surrender* was a dirty word — especially to young boys playing war. Whenever one group of boys was surrounded by the other, they had to surrender and it was shameful. So was saying "uncle" to the schoolyard bully. As an adult, however, I began to understand that when the Axis powers surrendered, we stopped bombing them (and, not coincidentally, helped them become global economic powers). Thus a new insight came aboard — when you surrender you stop hurting, whether you're on a schoolyard or a battlefield.

Or in an AA meeting. Continue to fight your disease and you lose; give up and surrender the fight and you become one of the million and a half Americans who are winners in AA. The book *Alcoholics Anonymous*, written in 1938 and published in 1939, rarely has the word "fight" in it. However, one notices the word *surrender* on page after page.

Acute illnesses such as the common cold are easy — take a couple of aspirin, get some rest and they will spontaneously go away. Chronic diseases such as alcoholism (and diabetes) require the sufferer to take continual action to keep them in remission. Likewise, rather than sitting around and not drinking, AA suggests *action:* turning off the television and going to a meeting; greeting the alcoholics who are there; exchanging telephone numbers; hearing and watching members who display the kind of attributes you want and asking one of them (usually a member of the same gender) to be a sponsor; sharing your story (if you choose to) of "what it was like, what happened, and what it's like now;" reaching out to help a newly-recovering alcoholic. Not for nothing is AA called a *support* group.

Those coming into recovery also notice that AA is methodical — it has adapted a systematic procedure, the hallmark of which is consistency, discipline and proven techniques. It is also sustained, on-going and habitual. That's a fancy way of saying that AA works because it provides structure and is based on proven recovery methods followed by others in the meeting and by the millions of those who have already recovered.

Your alcoholic probably understands the concept of car insurance, but he might not be aware that a personal program of recovery is based on the very same principle. As an example, if he buys a new car, chances are great that the very next thing he does is to buy car insurance. He knows well that at some point during the next few years or so, something undesirable will happen to that car — the law of averages says so. He knows he must share the risk of owning the car with someone else. If he doesn't and he loses, he loses big. He ends up making payments on something that's rusting in a junk yard.

A methodical program of recovery is to an alcoholic what insurance is to a new car owner. If your alcoholic is serious about his new-found sobriety, with the next breath he'll tell you that he's also invested in a recovery group like Alcoholics Anonymous. He knows that in the coming weeks, months and years, his sobriety will be tested. If he has learned to share the risk of relapse with those in the AA fellowship, chances are he'll pass the test with flying colors. If he loses because he has no "AA insurance," he loses big.

If your alcoholic enjoys one particular meeting — and there are hundreds of meetings each week in larger cities — chances are it's held each day or each week. Each time she attends, and many enjoy as many meetings as they can each week, she will be reminded that she's still powerless (but not helpless) over alcohol and other mood-altering chemicals. By talking and listening to others she'll also remind herself of how good she has it now that she's sober. Regular meetings, carrying the message of recovery, calling to mind her last bout with alcohol — these are signatures of a methodical program of recovery without which your alcoholic may insidiously slip back to her old playmates, her old playgrounds and her old disease which may put her behind bars, in a psychiatric institution or a cemetery.

Another way of thinking about Twelve-Step meetings is that they provide what American society cannot provide: a "container" for alcoholism. Swiss psychiatrist Dr. Carl Jung's treatment of former Rhode Island state senator Rowland Hazard in Zurich during the early 1930s was regarded by AA co-founder Bill Wilson as the spark that lit what came to be Alcoholics Anonymous. Jung believed that early societies ultimately learned to "contain" the use of mood-altering chemicals (wine, tobacco, peyote, etc.) through societal taboos, rites and religious traditions. America's modern, fragmented, more secular society lacks such containers. As a result, thought Jung, alcohol is used by alcoholics in an "uncontained" manner which wreaks emotional havoc and weakens society. Through their faith in a vital spiritual experience, modern Twelve-Step groups contain the use of alcohol while their concurrent group experience transforms failed individual efforts to stop drinking into a successful, collective effort toward achieving abstinence and emotional maturity.

Jung also believed that men and women make spiritual progress only by continually confronting their often beneficial but elusive *shadow* sides. Likewise, AA strongly suggests that the dark disease of alcoholism be accepted, embraced and healed by continuously discussing it with sponsors, other group members and, especially, by helping newly-recovering alcoholics.

It is impossible to overestimate the role that talking has upon a person's ability to confront his shadow side and change. For centuries, the Catholic Church has understood the benefits of vocalized confession and Sigmund Freud's "talking cure" is the focus of modern psychotherapy. Yale's Harold Bloom, in his book, *The Western Canon*, defended Shakespeare as central to all western literature chiefly because he allowed many of his tragic characters the capacity to "self-overhear" their own great soliloquies and become ennobled. Likewise, Twelve-Step groups (whether they realize it or not) encourage members to talk about their disease so they may "overhear themselves" and lay a strong foundation for change.

The disease of alcoholism is progressive, the process of denial is progressive, and recovery from alcoholism must also be progressive. We have already learned that the progressive nature of alcoholism means that it worsens if your alcoholic drinks or if he is abstinent. If he becomes a member of AA and slowly gets back health, self-respect, family, friends and employment, should it be surprising that the sobriety that brought this about must be protected with greater and greater vigilance?

How much recovery is needed? As they say in program, "it takes what it takes." For some, one or two regular meetings of AA per week (plus work with a sponsor and with sponsees) is sufficient. Others may need more meetings, more work with a sponsor and sponsees. Still others, however, may need structure to the point of milieu therapy. Being in a support group takes commitment — and the same commitment must be there during times of wealth and material success as when there's poverty and disappointment.

Recovery is also: (1) done best when the alcoholic's enabling system is in a concurrent recovery program; (2) ongoing, meaning it doesn't stop; (3) learning to think beyond the simple act of picking up the drink; (4) learning how to keep the brain from antagonizing what is in the heart; (5) just as serious and habitual as the disease of alcoholism itself!

AA's greatest legacy is its ability to gather hurting people together within a context of spirituality and mutual support. Dr. Jung and others recognized that the addictive use of alcoholic spirits seemed to be a malady that only spirituality could remedy — *Spiritus contra spiritum* (spirit against spirit) was the way he liked to put it.

Spirituality is indicated for those with alcoholism because it's a good tool for reducing the ego and its need to control. It may be safer to say that what is indicated for alcoholism is humility (ego deflation at depth) and that spirituality is the best way to get it and keep it. If that means that God is superfluous but faith in God is not — then let it be. AA has never contributed an iota of evidence of God's existence, but AA's insistence on ego deflation at depth (humility) has kept millions of people sober. The Rev. Thomas A. Dorsey said in the film *Say Amen, Somebody* that "If you don't know God, you've got to start all over."

What is a spiritual experience? Anything that proves to a person that he's essentially powerless. When an alcoholic first understands — after many vain attempts — that he cannot recover by himself, that is a spiritual experience. When an alcoholic utters the words, "God help me," that is a spiritual experience. When an alcoholic calls a sponsor, works with another alcoholic or walks into an AA meeting — newly sober or as an AA old-timer — that too is to acknowledge that her disease is stronger than she is and that only a Power Greater than herself will keep it in check. Obviously, I don't believe that a lack of spirituality makes one alcoholic, but I agree with Dr. Jung that this disease is a malady that can only be treated by socialization and an introduction to the spiritual world.

Chapter 10

Frequently Asked Questions

Loved ones and family members whose lives are affected by another's alcoholism can be expected to enter a counseling office or treatment center needing answers. It was always my habit to make a note of these "frequently asked questions" and I share them now. These answers are somewhat general; readers who need more specific answers are urged to contact the National Council on Alcoholism and Drug Dependence.

What if I'm asked to get involved in my loved one's treatment?

It has been stated several times that alcoholism touches not only the alcoholic but nearly everyone else in his "system" (family, friends, loved ones, church, workplace). So delicate is this system that therapists often need metaphors to describe it: an intricate Flying Wallendas-type high-wire act; a suspended mobile where the touch of a single part moves the whole. Some members of this system (family, friends, etc.) may understand the alcoholism for what it is. Others (church, workplace, etc.) may not; all they know is that something is clearly wrong with Joe.

Appreciating that alcoholism is a family disease, today's behavioral health centers use family programs to heal family systems. Certain high-dollar, green-campus type treatment centers offer such a comprehensive family program that significant others admit themselves right along with their alcoholic. Other modestly-priced ones may offer evening programs, two, three or four nights per week. AA's family component, so to speak, is Al-Anon Family Groups. But the goal is the same: to offer everyone in the system the honesty, communication skills and emotional maturity that recovery demands.

Many loved ones and family members attend such family programs having already given hospital admitting staff unspoken instructions to "Fix her." They'll come to learn that even if their alcoholic totally embraces recovery, to be "fixed," as it were, she might ultimately return to a family or workplace system that remains "broken." By broken, I mean where members of the system continue to keep secrets and refuse to own their feelings and behaviors. They may even sabotage a member's recovery by continuing to deny that she has a problem or by resenting the fact that she's no longer the distracted, easily-manipulated, irresponsible, blame-magnet she recently was.

Some balk at attending, saying, "He's the problem, why do you need me?" That's okay; most do. Others may fear they're walking, like Gene Autry perhaps, into a classic ambush where they will be pounced upon by their loved one and his therapist and publicly denounced as the real cause of the drinking. Still others might look forward to a family program as a chance to demonstrate the martyrdom they've suffered over the years.

Despite the fact that participation in a family therapy program makes most people fearful, it does provide an opportunity for clear discourse with an alcoholic without the yelling and the accusations. The therapist's job is to be fair to both sides so that truth, not what has long passed for truth, may prevail. The therapist will act as a traffic cop, a referee, a sifter of process from content, a model of appropriate behavior and a font of proven techniques to improve the way communication is carried out in post-rehab family life.

I have always thought that a good family therapist marries *families*. Think of it. Ordained clergy may unite couples in matrimony but few get to preside over the union of a committed, functional, multi-person, holistically healthy family. Instead of a gilded sanctuary there's a patient day room; rather than wedding rings, there's a circle of chairs; in place of a Bible or Torah, there's a well-thumbed AA or Al-Anon book; rather than punch and a three-tiered wedding cake there are left-over snacks and a Mr. Coffee that's long overdue for a cleaning; rather than tears of joy there are sobs of frustration; in place of a congregation of the freshly-scrubbed there are tired-looking, often exhausted persons who may not know where they're headed but know what's not acceptable anymore.

But make no mistake, a wonderful marriage can be made from such humble surroundings. Perhaps a far better one than the original which cost thousands and was based on pie-in-the-sky. If all the members of this unique wedding approach it with the respect that it demands, take their vows of recovery seriously, start listening, stop blaming each other, stop their enabling and remember that love is not an emotion but a series of choices based on the well-being of another, they may, more or less, live happily ever after.

What should I know about children of alcoholics?

Bill Clinton, Ronald Reagan, Gordon McRae, Carol Burnett and Chuck Norris all have one thing in common — they are children of alcoholics (COAs) just like one out of every five American children.

Just a few years ago, it was assumed that an alcoholic parent had to get sober before his child could get help. Today, it's understood that a COA can get help at any time. It was also assumed that a COA had to be identified and "labeled" so that proper attention could be paid to her. Today, thanks partly to work with attention-deficit/hyperactivity disorder (ADHD), it's known that such labeling may stigmatize children and make them "diagnosis victims."

It was even assumed that most COAs become alcoholic; yet around 60% do not. What's more, it seems that many COAs have a surprising amount of resiliency. "Children of the Garden Island" which appeared in the April, 1989 issue of *Scientific American*, points out how attachment to at least one loving, accepting caregiver can help children become resilient.

The garden island is Kauai on the northwest end of the Hawaiian chain, 100 miles west of Honolulu. There, beginning in 1954, author Emmy E. Werner studied how children of various cultures triumphed over physical disadvantages and deprived childhoods. Werner singled out 201 children from 698 who had moderate to severe reproductive stress, chronic poverty, parents with severely limited education, alcoholism in one or both parents, divorce and/or mental illness. These she termed "high-risk."

To her surprise, the author found that a third of these 201 high-risk children (72 to be exact) were highly resistant to their biological stress and harsh family environment and were resilient to the point where they went on to "develop healthy personalities, stable careers and strong interpersonal relations."

Among the biological (Nature) factors these children had going for them, according to Werner, were: temperaments that elicited positive responses from family members and strangers; a fairly-high activity level; a low degree of excitability and distress; a high degree of sociability; an ability to use their few talents effectively.

Among their positive environmental (Nurture) factors were: at least one caretaker (regular baby-sitter, aunt/uncle, older sibling) from whom they received *positive attention and unconditional love during their first years of life*; a family of fewer than four children; a space of at least two years between the observed child and his/her siblings; an ability to recruit emotional support outside of the family (from teachers, etc.); an ability to make school a refuge from family dysfunction; and habitual use of established institutions (YMCA, YWCA, church, school band, etc.).

The only gender difference Werner noticed was that resilient girls seemed to have assumed responsibility for a younger sibling when mother worked and dad was absent; and resilient boys seemed to be first born sons who had regular assigned chores. After 30 years, Werner reported that 44% of the 72 former high-risk children described themselves as happy, compared to only 10% of 129 low-risk kids.

Should alcoholics drink near-beer or near-wine?

Prior to the development and aggressive marketing of new brands of so-called "non-alcoholic" beers such as Hamms N.A., Miller Sharp's, Coors Cutter, O'Doul's and St. Pauli N.A., the debate over whether the consumption of so-called near-beers posed a threat to sobriety was little more than a murmur. Today, however, with massive advertising campaigns for such products (due ironically to the response of the brewing industry to consumers who desire to drink less or not at all), alcoholics must confront the near-beer dilemma as never before.

Near-beers were created during Prohibition to give beer aficionados the flavor and texture of real beer — the sale of which was illegal in that "great experiment" of the 1920s and 30s. The look, taste and package design of today's near-beers have become so sophisticated that they mimic the real thing to the point of confusion.

Alcoholics are never encouraged by serious therapists or support groups to buy and consume near-beer. This attitude exists for a number of reasons: First, you must visit a liquor store or liquor counter of a supermarket in order to buy it. And that's a slippery place for recovering alcoholics. Second, if you look closely at the label, you'll notice that each bottle contains a slight amount of alcohol. Third, the look, feel and taste of near-beer (or near-wine) might provide the alcoholic with too much near-reality. He might consciously or subconsciously expect a kind of high. Failing to find it could set him off on a search for the real thing. Some call the use of near-beer by alcoholics as "mental masturbation."

The argument for near-beer and near-wine when carried to a logical extreme envisions the use of near-vodka, near-Scotch and near-bourbon. Or how about a recovering cocaine user snorting lines of powdered sugar? — near-cocaine, as it were. Sound absurd? Of course it does. The same for near-beer and near-wine for an alcoholic.

All those who truly desire recovery (and not just near-sobriety) will be smart to leave the stuff alone. Non-alcoholic beer and wine is for, well — *non-alcoholics.*

Why can some people stop by themselves?
Good question. Perhaps you're asking this because you have, say, an uncle who stopped drinking some months or years ago, but your husband, try as he might, can't seem to repeat that success. I honestly have no idea why this happens other than to speculate that the pain of your uncle's drinking got to be greater than the discomfort of stopping.

Maybe he was not alcoholic and his drinking wasn't all that important to him. Or perhaps he started going to a church that frowns on the use of alcohol. Whatever the reason, it's clear that some people can stop while others can't. But remember, not drinking is being "dry." All too often, that means a person has stopped the "alcohol" but continues the "ism." In other words, your uncle may not be making behavioral and attitudinal changes associated with recovery to ensure that his life is filled with worthwhile activities instead of ones that cause pain and suffering.

What effect does alcohol have on the elderly?

A powerful one. As the body ages, the brain's susceptibility to the depressant effects of alcohol increases. Also, metabolism slows down and less water is retained in the cellular structure. When an older adult drinks alcohol it remains in the body for a longer period of time (longer than the usual one-ounce-per-hour rate of alcohol metabolism) and at a higher concentration than in a younger person. Thus even small amounts of alcohol can cause problems. Those much heralded two "moderate" drinks may be dangerous — especially when used in combination with prescription pills.

Elderly alcoholics are of two basic types: Typical alcoholics who have simply grown older; and those who perhaps drank socially for many years only to develop so-called "late-onset" alcoholism as they encountered the normal physiological changes of aging. (One method of preventing late-onset alcoholism is through the awareness of risk factors).

Women are more likely to develop late-onset alcoholism than men. And because many doctors fail to show sensitivity to women's health issues (or to older people for that matter), older women are more likely to be prescribed potentially addicting pharmaceuticals such as sleeping pills, tranquilizers and narcotic painkillers.

Treatment of elderly alcoholics must show sensitivity to their issues of retirement, relocation, death or illness of a spouse or adult child, confusion, forgetfulness, depression, grief, existential angst and their less-than-charitable definition of the word "alcoholic."

Therapists who practice with elderly populations often report that the biggest danger facing the elderly is the attitude and ignorance of family members: "At her age, what could it matter?" or "It's the only pleasure he has left." It's important to remember that alcoholism strips older adults of dignity, choice, reason and memory while devastating the physical body.

Wendy Adams of the Medical College of Wisconsin/Milwaukee reported in the September, 1993 issue of the *Journal of the American Medical Association* that the rate of hospitalization among people over 65 is greater for alcoholism than for heart attacks — and their care costs taxpayers more than $223 million per year. Also, the rate of hospital admissions of the elderly because of alcohol-related illnesses range from a low of 19 per 10,000 in Arkansas to 77 per 10,000 in Alaska. Adams wrote that alcohol should be considered as a factor among elderly patients when there are signs of liver disease, unexplained changes in mental function or stomach/intestinal problems.

Will my alcoholic be placed in treatment groups with drug addicts?

In my opinion, addicts and alcoholics should be co-mingled in process groups to remove their "terminal" uniqueness. Any therapist can tell you that alcoholics, heroin shooters, meth-heads and prescription pill droppers have a tendency to believe they are unique as a group and their needs are special. Alcoholics often look down their reddened noses at addicts, regarding them as common thieves and street punks. Likewise, cocaine snorters often look down their deviated-septums at alcoholics, regarding them as wimps who spend their lives taking the cross-town bus when, for a line of coke or two, they could hail the Space Shuttle. And the older, tranquilizer connoisseur may look down her physician-sculpted nose at all other addicts, regarding them as assorted low-lifes who simply misunderstand her special need for "mother's little helpers." By co-mingling these addicts in the same process group, each will come to learn that all their drugs worked for a while, stopped working and then plunged each into what St. John of the Cross termed a "dark night of the soul."

Alcoholics in co-mingled groups will also slam the door on any cocaine addict who believes he can successfully drink; likewise, a pot addict will soon set straight an alcoholic who's tempted to try the "marijuana maintenance" program.

Should treatment centers have separate process groups for women?

A therapy group for women only, so the argument goes, provides an embarrassment-free climate for confronting issues (incest, sexual trauma, bulimia, etc.) that women might not want to share with men. However, for me this has the odor of sexism and insinuates that men don't have issues (impotence, domestic violence, being gang raped) they would have difficulty sharing with women.

The function of the modern process group is to teach the art of risk taking. A man or woman learns to take risks in the safety of a small therapeutic circle and later with a Twelve-Step group. If needed, a woman may wish to do face-to-face therapy with her counselor and perhaps share her past with a female roommate prior to taking a larger risk with her treatment group. But a separate group for women will destroy group unity, play into her notion that she's unique and imply that alcohol is not an equal opportunity destroyer.

Women who take their risks only with other women may also deny men the privilege of practicing empathy and taking responsibility for their own pre-rehab behaviors which may include domestic violence, sexual harassment and sexual assault.

Is there a relationship between alcoholism and other issues affecting women?

Therapists are aware that a relationship exists in many women between alcoholism, childhood sexual abuse and eating disorders. So common is this terrible trio that if a woman seeks treatment for two of the issues, careful questioning will often uncover the third. The likelihood of the third being present is uncanny. No one knows why this relationship exists although the answer may be found when more is understood about the relationship between trauma and alcoholism.

Careful questioning of female clients might also uncover past abortions which often play a large role in keeping them caught in a guilt spiral. Whether one condones abortions or not, they do tend to produce issues that women drink over.

Does so-called "aversion" or "desensitization" therapy work with alcoholism?

I am not ready to give an unqualified no, but I have great reservations.

Aversion therapy is based on the same Pavlovian psychology which a century ago conditioned dogs to salivate at the sound of a bell. Aversion therapists condition an alcoholic to associate consumption of alcohol with nausea and revulsion. The same principle is used by parents who buy a large bag of candy knowing, perhaps, that their four-year-old sugar junkie will get sick and stop eating it. One problem. The typical alcoholic has hundreds of experiences with revulsion and it never seems to slow down his drinking. That's why they call it *alcoholism*. Most inebriates will admit that while they had their head stuck in a toilet bowl throwing up today's booze, they were thinking about tomorrow's. Perhaps a person may use aversion therapy to remain abstinent for a short while — if that's all he wants. But careful follow-up with a Twelve-Step group will treat the whole person, not just the drinking problem.

The second Pavlovian-based treatment is called "Cue exposure desensitization therapy." Its idea is to expose the ex-drinker to stimuli (shot glasses, beer steins, taverns and other drinking environments). By learning not to act on such stimuli, it is thought that the drinker's craving will slowly extinguish and his confidence will soar. It's not unusual for newly recovering alcoholics — who have never heard of cue exposure — to "test themselves" by hanging around in bars. They'll tell you that they don't want to drink, they just want to shoot pool. Most therapists and sober alcoholics don't buy this. Bars and taverns are slippery places, full of slippery people. Cue exposure for alcoholics makes as much sense as a recovering sex addict hanging around a porno book store.

What is meant by "Collapse of the alibi system?"

The lowest level of the left hand or "downward progression" side of the Jellinek Chart is where one encounters this condition. Alcoholics are well-known for making excuses about their drinking; their disease is an insidious one and they have plenty of time to linger over their composition. Early in an alcoholic's drinking career these alibis are watertight. "I hadn't eaten all day and the cocktails got to me." Later on, as the disease progresses, the alcoholic, whether handicapped by dementia or apathy, constructs and maintains these alibis in a less precise manner: "I drink too much because you're always nagging at me." By the time the alcoholic finds himself in the trough of the Jellinek Chart, he's no longer bothering with alibis or fictions (or even hope itself):

"Hell yes I'm intoxicated. What did you expect? I'm nothing but a drunk!"

One way to collapse this alibi system sooner is by collapsing the enabling system so even seemingly good alibis are no longer accepted. An alibi is successful only if the listener actually believes it.

How effective are pharmaceuticals for alcoholism?

There are two types of pills available to help the alcoholic stop drinking and remain abstinent. The oldest, Antabuse (disulfiram), became available in 1948 as the first medication cleared by the FDA for the relief of alcoholism. Antabuse is available by prescription only and has proved effective in making problem drinkers think twice about drinking. Antabuse works on the medically-sound premise that it's not the alcohol *per se* that gives the drinker a terrible hangover. The hangover is caused by a metabolite of alcohol called acetaldehyde. When one drinks, the alcohol journeys to the liver and exits in the form of acetaldehyde. One feels ill until this liver metabolite begins leaving the body through the kidneys. Antabuse, however, prevents or drastically blocks the reabsorption and elimination of this metabolite leaving the drinker with a perpetual hangover (flushing, rapid heartbeat, nausea, headache, etc.). The theory is that the threat of a bad enough sick spell will deter drinking. Taking Antabuse on a daily basis means the consumer had better not drink for a few days after the last pill is taken or he might soon be praying for death. However, if no beverage alcohol, alcohol-based mouthwashes, cough medicines or after-shave lotions are consumed or applied topically to the skin, the constituent chemicals of Antabuse remain inert.

Antabuse is formulated to be an aid to sobriety, not a formal program of recovery. Those who take it will one day discontinue taking it and will need to be planted feet-first in a support group. However, dually-diagnosed alcoholics (post-traumatic stress or bipolar disorder, etc.) may need to continue taking Antabuse while they progress through psychotherapy. Compliance with a daily Antabuse regimen may be monitored by checking the urine for the metabolite diethylamine.

For Antabuse to be successful, an alcoholic must understand its action and have a good grasp of its risks and benefits; his prescribing physician must test him for an allergic reaction and make certain that he is well enough to survive a worst-case scenario of drinking while on Antabuse; his therapist must view the voluntary taking of Antabuse as a healthy commitment to sobriety; and the spouse (who may wish to monitor its consumption) will come to understand that his use of Antabuse will remove her nagging notion that he's taking a drink on the sly.

A newer pharmaceutical is called ReVia (pronounced "reh VEE uh") and was release by the FDA in January of 1995. ReVia (Naltrexone) is manufactured by DuPont Merck and is a proven chemical for narcotic addiction that has been found to have applications for alcoholism. Naltrexone is a narcotic antagonist, meaning that it essentially undoes everything that a hit of opium, heroin or morphine is designed to do. If you were to show up at a hospital emergency room for heroin overdose, Naltrexone would be used to render the heroin inert. That's why it's referred to as an antagonist. When DuPont Merck began testing Naltrexone for alcoholism, it seemed to reduce craving in abstinent patients and block the reinforcing effects of alcohol in patients who drank. ReVia seems to have promise in reducing relapse rates of newly-sober alcoholics. It is a proven agent but it is not a "magic bullet." It won't cure alcoholism. Anyone who tells you otherwise is a charlatan, a profiteer or is ignorant about alcoholism. It's used in conjunction with professional psycho/social therapy and follow-up Twelve-Step support. ReVia is available only through prescription.

The future might provide truly "high tech" pharmaceuticals such as genetic markers, third-generation selective serotonin reuptake inhibitors (SSRI's), drugs useful for genetic reengineering, drugs that address collateral depression and anxiety, and sophisticated psychoactive drugs that actually repair internal organs.

What should I know about post-treatment-center surgery?

Because active alcoholics rarely darken the door of a doctor, it's not uncommon for them to schedule much-overdue surgery immediately following a successful stay in rehab. This can be accomplished with a minimum of risk by securing a surgeon who is familiar with addiction (see the following question), explaining to him that you are a recovering alcoholic and by extension, that makes you addicted to mood-altering chemicals such as narcotic pain killers. If pain pills are needed, it may be better to hand them over to a concerned spouse or a fellow recovering alcoholic for dispensation as prescribed. When no more are needed, they should be disposed of.

Don't be like one of my patients who, when reciting her aftercare plan in front of a process group, casually mentioned that she would leave rehab and spend the very next day undergoing routine gynecological surgery. When quizzed by the group as to the wisdom of this move, she made it clear that she had given little thought to the risk of becoming addicted to so-called *solid* alcohol.

Is there a list of doctors who know about alcoholism?

The American Society of Addiction Medicine (ASAM) will provide, upon request, the names of ASAM members in your area. This assures you that the physician you retain maintains an interest in addictionology and has demonstrated knowledge and competency through written tests. Call 301-656-3920.

Do medical doctors have much experience with alcoholism?

They didn't in the past. However, medical schools are trying to update their curriculum to reflect the sobering truth that 40% of all hospital admissions (and nearly half of all trauma beds) are related to the misuse of alcohol and other drugs.

Thomas L. Delbanco, MD, writing in a recent *Journal of the American Medical Association*, says that physicians are often loathe to intervene in the alcoholism of a patient. This happens for several reasons. For instance, many physicians lack education as to the treatment of alcoholism. (He admits his first and only contact with alcoholism during medical school happened when a teaching pathologist held up a liver during an autopsy and announced, "Ladies and gentlemen, this is cirrhosis.")

Delbanco also points out that doctors have few, experienced addictionists to act as role models; often misconstrue a patient's denial as outright deceit; and are frustrated when their concern is taken as condemnation.

Doctors also: know that alcoholics rarely take their advice; don't like to bear ill tidings or stigmatize patients; are afraid that those they treat will disappear if they express concern; don't always like patients with chronic or recurring illness; and may be closet alcoholics or pill poppers themselves. Even if the patient is in agreement about alcoholism, the doctor may feel ill-equipped to manage recovery or endorse a specific treatment program.

Attempting to correct this situation, Hazelden New York, a 55-bed residential CD facility, trains medical residents to identify, diagnose and treat alcoholic and other drug dependent patients. Hazelden's Physicians in Residence Program is a five-day tour which combines authoritative lectures with hands-on experience.

On the first day, each resident is teamed with a patient with whom s/he works, shares meals and accompanies to therapy sessions, support groups and AA meetings. In this way, residents learn first-hand what pressures and stresses people face when trying to overcome their addictions.

Lectures comprising a crash course in addiction medicine fill out the remainder of the program. Topics include the physiology of addiction; denial; role of the physician; early intervention; assessment and diagnosis; psychotropic drugs and pain medication; dual diagnosis; the Twelve-Step recovery plan; treatment modalities; and factors leading to relapse. Hazelden directors say that patients are less stigmatized when doctors learn to treat alcoholism like any other disease and avoid becoming moralistic or punitive.

Is it okay to get AA meetings from Internet chat rooms?
You may be surprised to learn from this question that yes, AA meetings are available in cyberspace. Whether this is good or bad remains to be seen. Certainly, those who are what grandma called "bed-ridden" or "shut-in" may benefit from Internet AA. But hasn't alcoholism already been defined as a disease of isolation? And doesn't interaction between alcoholics through a computer keyboard seem to smack of isolation?

As Chapter 9 on *Recovery* made clear, AA suggests action: turning off the TV, putting on your jacket, driving to a meeting, parking your car and greeting fellow recovering alcoholics face-to-face. There, you exchange telephone numbers, hear and watch people who display the kind of attributes you want, ask one of them to be a sponsor and perhaps have coffee with them afterward. Your alcoholic simply cannot set up chairs, hug a newcomer, dry a tear, hold a hand, drink coffee, exchange a phone number, laugh at himself or eat anniversary cake on the Internet.

What kinds of problems do combat survivors face when recovering?

Much has been written about post-traumatic stress disorders (PTSD) that plague combat veterans and other trauma survivors. The condition is certainly not new. Toward the beginning of Act II, Scene III of Shakespeare's *King Henry IV* (First Part), the character of Lady Percy, a soldier's wife, so accurately describes husband Hotspur's PTSD symptoms that the passage could be lifted verbatim from the Bard's 400-year-old play and dropped into modern diagnostic manuals without changing a word.

When PTSD was noticed anew in the early 1970s, it was misdiagnosed as paranoid schizophrenia; in the late 1970s it was seen as manic-depression. In the early 1980s, however, the American Psychiatric Association formally recognized its diagnosis and PTSD was seen for what it always was, a condition that mimics virtually any psychiatric condition, a roadblock to assimilation back to civilian life, a life-threatening malady and, certainly, a barrier to full recovery from mood-altering chemicals.

Many of my NCADD clients who saw combat in Southeast Asia had two things in common: they used downers more or less exclusively (alcohol, pot, heroin, sedatives, tranquilizers, etc.) and seemed to have successfully coped with more familiar PTSD symptoms such as intrusive flashbacks, constant vigilance, numbness, mistrust, internalization of feelings, nightmares, assaultive episodes, survivor guilt and startle reactions. What kept them from true recovery seemed to be their adoption of the "Vietnam war veteran" as their sole identity. Seemingly stuck in an unpopular war, these veterans continued to dress in green military fatigues, sobbed at Memorial Day services and spent countless hours recalling combat experiences with fellow veterans.

Regardless of how many recovery options were presented to the veterans by the author, their path led to the same crossroads: either a commitment to true recovery or a life of booze and "negative support" groups. Sadly, many were unable to shun the path of beer and war stories and a "therapeutic window" was often permanently closed.

How compatible is Prozac with those recovering from alcoholism?

The much-maligned anti-depressant Prozac has been available by prescription since 1988 and there seems to be no major stumbling block to its use by recovering persons.

As a rule, non-alcoholics, after being stabilized on Prozac, may choose to return to drinking in moderation provided there are no adverse effects. It is never suggested, however, that alcoholics who take Prozac abandon their abstinence program. It's always good to tell your doctor, psychotherapist or psychologist if you regard yourself as an alcoholic and then pray that he or she understands addiction.

Those with liver disease are usually given low doses of Prozac as liver problems more than double the drug's half-life. Continued research is being done to see whether such anti-depressants can be used to reduce the craving for alcohol and other drugs such as cocaine.

How do employers find out about an employee's drinking problem?

Employers often believe they'll discover on-the-job drinking by finding bottles; this almost never happens. However, careful attention to productivity, absenteeism (especially on Mondays, Fridays and the day after payday), tardiness, and an occasional call from a worried or vengeful spouse, will provide the smoking gun that an employee is showing up at work impaired.

The philosophy behind modern-day Employee Assistance Programs (EAPs) is that good employees are an asset to the company and if they happen to be alcoholic, it makes sense to get them treatment so that the mutually beneficial work relationship continues. Decades ago, employers simply rooted out the alcoholics, hired others to replace them, and trained them at great expense only to discover that some of them, too, were alcoholic.

Federal law rightly says that employees may not be discharged because of a disease or disability such as alcoholism. However, they may be discharged for violating well-documented company policies regarding attendance, tardiness and productivity.

Companies have the ultimate "hammer" for formally intervening on an employee (see Chapter 7 on *Formally Intervening*). It will be difficult for your lover to ignore a compassionate but well-documented intervention which takes place in the human resources office and is attended by many of the company's top management staff.

Is alcoholism considered a mental health problem?

No. *Mental* health is a measurement of known (organic) or unknown (inorganic) psychiatric disorders. Alcoholism falls under the general category of *behavioral* health. In other words, alcoholism is about behaviors that result in physical, emotional, spiritual and legal problems. The aforementioned description of an alcoholic as *a person with a pathological problem who, once he chooses to start, finds it extremely difficult to stop drinking,* does not describe a strict medical condition or mental illness as much as it does a disease of behavior. Treatment for behavioral health problems concerns itself with modifying actions and learning newer, more acceptable coping skills.

With the passage in 1970 of the Comprehensive Alcohol Abuse and Alcoholism Prevention, Treatment and Rehabilitation Act (the Hughes Act), the disease aspect of alcoholism was made public policy and behavioral health became a distinct new field of health care. Treatment began to be covered by health insurance and chemical dependency treatment centers sprang up around the nation.

In the days before the proliferation of these behavioral health units most alcoholism treatment was provided by hospitals which dealt solely with psychiatric disorders. These so-called "psych" hospitals believed that it made clinical and economic sense to co-mingle alcoholics with others on the unit. This led to bewildered alcoholics sitting in process groups with highly-medicated psychiatric patients. Needless to say, this did not work. Alcoholism and psychiatric disorders are entirely different breeds of cat; to place alcoholics among the seriously mentally ill precludes the provision of proper treatment to both deserving segments. Today, psych hospitals have learned that tough lesson and smart consumers will ask hospital personnel prior to admission if it co-mingles its chemical dependency (CD) and psychiatric units.

The up-side of the modern psych hospital is that it uniquely understands how to treat the patient with a dual diagnosis (having both mental and behavioral health problems). This is good because their numbers in such hospitals are legion. It knows that some patients with mental illnesses (bipolar disorder, borderline personality disorder, for example) can successfully be treated with group therapy, while patients with schizophrenia are most often ill-equipped for the confrontation that such groups can generate.

The down-side is that the constant focus on an alcoholic's associated mental health issues (anxiety, mood and antisocial personality disorders, etc.) may hinder recovery by triggering so-called "med-seeking" behaviors and by playing into pre-existing feelings of uniqueness.

While there are many who are dually diagnosed, it is generally understood that alcoholics do not have a substantially greater incidence of mental illness than the general population. As has been discussed, mental illness does not *cause* alcoholism. If it did, all mentally ill persons would be alcoholic — a preposterous statement.

I hear people talk about therapists and about AA sponsors. What's the difference?

Therapists are formally-trained professionals who provide help to clients through face-to-face meetings or in "process" groups wherein a certain number of clients meet with therapists to discuss problems with their cognitive, affective and/or behavioral responses to certain life situations, i.e., their "process." Therapists are bound or sworn to published ethical codes; their relationships with patients or clients have been adjudicated and protected by a court of law; they make formal appointments; form mostly short-term relationships with clients; develop and follow treatment plans and measure treatment outcomes. Therapists do a limited amount of client follow-up or "wellness checks;" they maintain written records; are not bound by Twelve-Step Traditions and are not necessarily spiritually oriented. Therapists often use professionally-developed written or verbal tests to aid diagnosis; they attend to both voluntary and involuntary clients; treat secondary mental illnesses and basically practice out of compassion and for economic gain.

AA sponsors always work one-on-one with "sponsees;" are rarely formally trained; are neither bound nor sworn to published ethical codes; do not enjoy legally-protected sponsor/sponsee relationships; are available on demand; and often develop a close relationship with another AA member that lasts for decades. Sponsors don't draft treatment plans or measure outcomes. They do some follow-up with sponsees although they're careful not to "enable" them; they write nothing down; are bound informally by the 12 AA Traditions; are often highly spiritual; care little for formal diagnosis; work mainly with those who voluntarily go to AA; have neither the expertise nor an interest in treating a secondary mental illness; and provide time to others mainly in an effort to keep themselves sober.

Both therapists and AA sponsors have certain things in common: they generally believe that "it's the relationship that heals;" both will tell you the truth whether you like it or not; they value homework as a way of extending the session into the patient's or sponsee's outside life; refuse to set themselves up as money lenders, cab drivers or employers; help their clients and sponsees clarify the choices they must make; value insight and awareness; model appropriate behavior and basically try to help troubled people get more from life.

Isn't addiction just another name for compulsion?

A compulsion is a mostly subconscious behavior where a person acts totally against his own will (non-stop talking, repeated hand washing, etc.). There's no drug or drug-like agent involved and the person engaged in the compulsive behavior gets no euphoric "payoff" from it.

An addiction is a *conscious* activity which always involves a physical drug or a harmful activity (overeating, shopaholism, gambling, etc.) which provides the same arousal or tranquilizing effect of a drug. Alcoholics, for instance, often act against their own will ("I really want to drink but I know I shouldn't.") but their consumption of the first drink is always a conscious choice. Likewise, an addiction to food, shopping or gambling will kick in only when the addict begins to eat, shop or roll the dice. Once that initial activity is consciously started, stopping it will prove extremely difficult.

Must a good therapist have survived a personal bout with alcoholism?

Let's look at it this way. To correctly identify, diagnose and treat cancer, an oncologist needs extensive education, training, experience and licensure. But few would demand that she also be a cancer survivor.

Likewise, a good alcoholism therapist needs to be properly trained, educated and certified, but having personal experience with a drinking problem isn't always necessary. Granted, therapists with personal experience may show an empathy, sympathy and heightened sensitivity to the needs of their alcoholic clients. And granted, "entry level" patients/clients may feel more comfortable with someone who's "been there." But such therapists often have concurrent struggles with their own recovery which may be heightened by the stress of working in the alcoholism field. And who's to say that therapists without personal experience with alcoholism can't show the same compassion? Treatment centers which insist that therapists must be recovering alcoholics may unwittingly be playing into their patient's egotism or feelings of uniqueness. And any patient who announces that he simply can't get sober unless his therapist is an ex-drunk is putting conditions on his sobriety. In my experience, however, good therapists, whether recovering or not, have successfully processed their own personal issues and understand how the Twelve-Steps apply to their lives.

AA is right in pointing out that "only an alcoholic can help another alcoholic." But AA is not treatment, although many have great difficulty distinguishing the two.

Does relapse play a role in recovery?

Decades ago, getting drunk again was simply referred to as "getting drunk again." Today, the less-stigmatizing word "relapse" is used instead as it forces us to remember that relapse is not a single act (taking a drink) but a highly-personal *process* that must be identified and examined on a regular basis. In other words, taking a drink is not the *beginning* of relapse; it's the result of the insidious relapse process.

Preventing relapse is one of the major goals of treatment and self-help groups. Being educated in the fine art of relapse prevention necessitates (among other things) that one learn how to manage leisure time, adopt a methodical program of recovery, refrain from hanging around "slippery" people and recognize personalized "triggers" that start the buildup to the next drink. That next buildup must be anticipated; nothing must be left to chance. The alcoholic learns to get an AA sponsor and be accountable to him so that at least one other person knows where the alcoholic is going and why. He learns to check his motives with the sponsor. For instance, if he tells the sponsor he wants to go with friends to San Diego for the weekend, the sponsor may say, "If you're going to experience sober fellowship with other recovering persons and you want to go to the many beach AA meetings there, then that sounds like a good idea. However, if you're going back to old drinking haunts with old drinking buddies, you might do yourself a favor and stay home."

It has been the prevailing opinion that all relapses are bad. It's not surprising to see why. If one of the major tasks of treatment is to prevent relapse, shouldn't relapse be seen as evidence of treatment failure? Certainly, as we have seen, alcoholics cannot predict what they're going to do when they take the first drink. They may live or they may die. Because relapse places them in this danger zone, conventional wisdom says that relapses are never beneficial.

But let's consider this. If one treats as beneficial the many dozens of relapses *prior* to one's entry into treatment then why should all post-treatment relapses be considered as evidence of failure? Relapse wakes one up to pain and consequences whether it's done prior to or following treatment. Therapists and AA sponsors have all noticed that certain resistant alcoholics do seem to benefit from one last relapse following treatment or entrance into AA. No one should ever plan to relapse; no one should ever take relapse for granted; one should work a methodical program of recovery to prevent relapse. However, from the vantage of hindsight, it does appear that many seem to benefit from a "therapeutic relapse" but the trick is to try not to die or kill someone while doing it.

Another reason why relapsers shouldn't be ostracized is because relapse can carry with it a stigma of shame and failure. Those with little ego-strength may be pushed over the edge to suicide by assuming the shame of relapse. This is why it's important to not stigmatize anyone who relapses. Relapse can be part of the disease of alcoholism — although it *doesn't have to be* if a program of recovery is worked. Those who relapse should be quickly welcomed back to the fold with compassion and love.

What is euphoric recall?

Euphoric recall may be thought of as "romancing the high" and all persons bask in it to some extent. Some do it infrequently, some do it often. It's human nature for the mind to sort — like wheat from chaff — the pleasant from the painful aspects of a memory. The easiest way to explain this phenomenon is to remember when you dated (or married) that one special guy whom you swore to love forever. However, by the time your relationship was finished, you were yelling and throwing things at each other. You hated him and never wanted to see him again. Then, a few years later, you sit back and think of him. He was good looking, had a great body and when he wasn't drinking and moody, he was great fun. "Why did we ever break up?" you think to yourself. "Why don't I just give him a call?"

That's euphoric recall. You're recalling the euphoric or "good times" rather than the bad. Again, it's human nature. Through the years, you conveniently forgot that he used to stand you up for dates; that he would show up at your apartment with a bunch of his no-good friends; that he always seemed too busy to talk about where the relationship was headed; and he was always bumping into attractive women who seemed to know him. And you want all this back?

To the alcoholic, such recall is dangerous. Often, the alcoholic's mind strays back to his early days of drinking — the days when it may have been fun; when school chums met for a drink, when relationships with that special girl were cemented with a glass of wine. Yes, those were fun days, but they were 10 or 20 years ago. It's not therapeutic for the alcoholic to think about or glorify those times — they're gone forever. The alcoholic must confine his thinking to the *very last time* alcohol was consumed. That was the time that the car was wrecked, the harsh words were exchanged or the pushing and shoving began. There are many things recovering alcoholics must learn to avoid; euphoric recall is one of them.

Should I search my teenager's room for drugs?

For many parents, this is a question of Constitutional proportions. A noble debate touching on the Bill of Rights and its Right to Privacy.

Hogwash. Looking for drugs in your teen's room no more violates the Right to Privacy than a ban on talking in class violates Free Speech or the adoption of school uniforms violates First Amendment Rights of Expression. When did a parent's responsibility to ensure their teenager is healthy and drug-free become secondary to their teenager's "right" to sneak around and do mood-altering chemicals? Wanting to know what your daughter is hiding in her sock drawer is not about trust — it's about ensuring she doesn't get caught up in something that will take her youth or her life. To be sure, no parent likes the idea of searching the room of an adolescent for contraband and then dealing with the confrontation that inevitably follows. But often, conditions make it mandatory. Question: would you as a parent allow your 13-year-old to take off on a cross-country jaunt with a couple of friends? Of course not. You would intervene and put a stop to it. Likewise, if that same 13-year-old is being provided with alcohol and other drugs by those same friends, wouldn't you be willing to do everything in your power to stop it?

Prior to the search, however, it is important for the parents to know what they plan to do with the information should drugs or suspicious material be found. Does it mean addiction? Should the youth get treatment? Is it truly drugs? Parents must first seek information from adolescent treatment centers or NCADD affiliates lest they stigmatize their son or daughter and embarrass themselves by overreacting to a problem that may or may not be there.

If drugs or suspicious material is found, make sure that you let a clinic or treatment center advise you as to its ultimate disposition. Don't jump in your car with a bag of stash, drive to a treatment center and say, "Hey, taste this and tell me what it is!" The treatment center probably employs recovering addicts and for you to shove a bag of crystal methamphetamine or cocaine under their nose will not be an aid to their recovery. Nor will it endear you to a policeman who stops you for speeding and asks why you have drugs in the car.

What works with adolescents?

The treatment of choice for adolescents is the carefully negotiated contract between them and the adults in their lives (assuming they have such). This is done for many reasons, chief of which is the fact that much of what adolescents do is related to power. "I'll see if I can't get you to do things my way and if so, I win." So caught up in this are most adolescents that their behavior is unfathomable until placed in the context of a power struggle.

An effective way to reach adolescents is to show them how alcohol and other drugs take away their newly-found power. Adolescents seem to instinctively understand that when they begin to get the power they crave (or the driver's license they want) alcohol and other drugs will take it from them post haste.

Adolescents are surprised and pleased when they sit in a counselor's office and help *negotiate* an arrangement or plan of action which will determine the actions of their family. By being allowed to negotiate with adults, the teenager's craving for power is satisfied and their "buy-in" to the contract is ensured.

Contracts are negotiated by a third party — usually a counselor familiar with the process. She will begin by going over the rules: "Everyone's here to negotiate; there's to be no grandstanding or bargaining in ill faith." Once negotiated, the contract will stand for a specified period of time as agreed upon by the family. Afterward, it will be renegotiated, perhaps with more leeway for the adolescent — if the leeway has been earned.

The counselor will then describe the items of the contract which are non-negotiable: items such as no drug use, drug possession, drug T-shirts, drug talk or drug paraphernalia; the right to search the room and take a drug test when asked. This is entered under the column entitled: "What the adolescent will do." Other mentions will include standards for school grades, homework and curfew times. The parents may want to negotiate these last three items. If so, the bargaining starts:

Parents: We believe that curfew should be at 8 pm on school nights and 9 pm on Friday and Saturday nights.
Adolescent: No way! I like 8:30 weekdays and 10 pm weekends.

Parents: We're willing to compromise a little on this. Let's say that we start by keeping 8 pm on school nights but switch to, say, 9:30 on weekends. If the contract is adhered to for the first six months, maybe we'll come back together and think about 8:30 on school nights.
Adolescent: Cool!

Of course he thinks it's cool — he just negotiated something in his favor from an adult. How grownup! Is it any wonder that he'll proudly display this on the refrigerator door and adhere to its provisions?

Along with a column entitled "What the adolescent will do" will be two other columns: "What the parents agree to do" and "What both parties agree to do." Among the items on the former might be that the parents agree to refrain from nagging the adolescent. An item on the latter might be that both parties will endeavor to tone down the yelling.

To ensure compliance with the contract, sanctions are levied. If the adolescent fails to comply with one of the *negotiable* items, the curfews may jump a half-hour earlier until such time that compliance is reached. Violation of a *non-negotiable* item like alcohol or other drug use/possession is another matter. Some parents and counselors draft the contract with the provision that if chemicals are possessed or used the first time, the door of the adolescent's room is removed from its hinges and stored in the garage for a month. (Definitely uncool!) A second violation may mean mandatory admission into an adolescent drug treatment unit. Refusal to take a drug test by the teen will be regarded as an admission of drug use. The contract is then signed by all parties and displayed in a conspicuous, but confidential, place.

Do those in Greek fraternities really drink more than non-Greeks?

They do if they live in the frat house. Cheryl Presley, Ph.D., in her book *Alcohol and Drugs on American College Campuses*, reported that frat house residents admit to an average of 20.3 drinks per week compared with 7.5 by non-Greeks and Greeks who live in dorms or off-campus. Frat house residents also: drink earlier than other students (87% drank prior to age 18); hear more criticism because of how they drink (16.3% vs. 12% of all students); have more booze-related health consequences (blackouts, nausea, vomiting, hangovers, injuries); have more injuries due to drinking; receive more DUIs and suffer more academic consequences (poor test scores, missed classes, etc.).

How is alcoholism diagnosed?

There are many ways of insinuating that alcoholism exists. One may *self-diagnose* as is done by many thousands of Twelve-Step group members. One may consult a list of symptoms in a diagnostic manual and *conclude* that the illness is present if a person has an arbitrary number of these symptoms. One may *suggest* that a person "in my opinion seems to display symptoms that are associated with the disease of alcoholism" — as is done by less formally-educated counselors who may be legally or ethically prevented from making a formal diagnosis.

More controversial are the less discussed political, financial and medicalized diagnoses. Alcoholism is hardly ever seen as having a *political* component until it becomes understood that once such a diagnosis is made, public assistance checks may have to be written to cover treatment and aftercare under the Americans With Disabilities Act. Prominent psychiatrist R. D. Laing (*The Politics of Experience*) has already warned about politicizing the diagnosis of mental illness by a dominant society which, in its own madness, becomes intolerant of unconventional or aberrant behavior.

Diagnoses become *financialized* in much the same way. Major insurance carriers have a stake in whether or not a policyholder is diagnosed as alcoholic — especially if his policy underwrites treatment. Fewer diagnosed alcoholics means fewer reimbursements and a more attractive bottom line.

Jerome Kroll, in his book *The Challenge of the Borderline Patient*, says "Physicians, jurists and legislators tend to *medicalize* many conditions which bear a dubious relationship to disease and illness." He cites as examples such ordinary life conditions as backaches, tension headaches, insomnia, obesity and blood pressure readings above an arbitrary level. Social model alcoholism therapists have noticed that alcoholism, an "orphan" disease whose underlying pathology (unlike cancer) is unclear, is slowly becoming medicalized (nature abhors an "orphan" as much as a vacuum). So much so that if the behavioral health field continues to look the other way, highly-capitalized managed care systems (public or private) will proclaim it just another medical problem that only doctors can treat. Social model treatment centers will then be required to have doctors and nurses on staff and to somehow conform to expensive medical procedures.

What's the toughest age to diagnose?
It is difficult to diagnose the disease of alcoholism without stigmatizing someone. The diagnosis of cancer or diabetes does not carry the emotional baggage of an alcoholism diagnosis. Cancer and diabetes are associated with the victimization of a person; alcoholism with what a person seems to have done to himself.

Diagnosis of alcoholism is certainly stigmatizing with the young and the elderly. The toughest diagnostic sessions I

faced as a counselor were those conducted with someone between 17-22 years old or in their last few years of life.

The young are usually free from mom and dad for the
first time and may even have gone to college and joined a
fraternity. So caught up are they in the "Beer = Fun" equation incessantly pitched on campuses by breweries that they
guzzle beer by the hour. They then run afoul of school codes
or public laws and are required to visit an alcoholism counselor for diagnosis. Clearly, the young person did get a DUI
and was later found asleep on the frat house lawn. Clearly,
he's drinking way too much. Clearly, he's what Plato had in
mind 2,400 years ago when he warned about mixing wine
with testosterone ("It is wrong to add fire to fire."). But is he
an alcoholic?

One of the problems with trying to diagnose youth is that
drinking is often prevalent. (I am tempted to use the term
"age-appropriate" but refrain as it seems to condone drinking.) What if he, like many, merely sows wild oats in college
and spends the rest of his life socially drinking? Estimate the
percentage of college students who drink too much (50%-
60%?) and then remind yourself that only around 10% of all
adult Americans are alcoholic. What happened to all those
college students? It appears they drank too much in college
and then stopped. Call it peer pressure if you want, call it
"aggressive experimentation" if you like, but can you call it
alcoholism? Rather than stigmatize a 19-year-old, I usually
stopped short of diagnosing alcoholism in favor of calling it
"a clear example of alcohol abuse which may be solved by
education and practicing the techniques of peer group resis-
tance."

The elderly were usually brought in for diagnosis by
family members. They were tough to diagnose not because
symptoms weren't crystal clear. These were marvelous and
highly resilient men and women who had been through two
world wars and a major economic depression. When they

learned the word "alcoholic" it meant a bum on the street —
a skid-row denizen who ambulated about drinking from a
paper bag and muttering to himself. These aged folks had
spent at least 65-70 years with that definition and to tag
them with it, the way a wildlife biologist tags a bear, seemed
unfair and pointless. They and their family were, however,
encouraged to seek out their own support groups and were
provided with information on maintaining abstinence and
permanently collapsing their enabling system.

When is it time for a formal diagnosis of secondary issues?
Far too many clients show up for counseling and take part in
this kind of dialogue:

Client: I've been sober for a week and yesterday I found out I
    was manic-depressive.
Counselor: (Gulps loudly and turns somewhat white).
Client: I went to the other therapist I'm required to see by my
    probation officer and when I told him about all those
    mood swings I've been having, he said, "Sounds like a
    bipolar disorder." So, now I'm on medication.
Counselor: Did you tell him you consider yourself alcoholic
    and that most detoxing or newly-sober alcoholics de-
    scribe themselves as being on an emotional roller
    coaster?
Client: I guess I forgot.

There seems to be no hard and fast rule as to how long a
newly-recovering alcoholic should wait before he seeks psychotherapy for secondary issues. Emergencies, of course,
demand immediate attention. However, mental health professionals simply cannot diagnose secondary issues
(depression, etc.) until an alcoholic has been sober for a
while. Some psychologists and psychiatrists maintain that
their non-emergency clients must be sober for at least three

months. If not, they know they're being asked to diagnose and treat little more than a bottle of alcohol.

Wouldn't it be easier to sell the idea of treatment to someone if abstinence weren't a treatment goal?

Undoubtedly. In a fantasy world, treatment centers would teach problem drinkers to drink in moderation. Thus, such centers would pack them in, marketing departments would be happy, heads would be on beds and drinkers could still hang on to their booze. In the real world, however, alcoholics know intuitively (while they may not want to admit it) that treatment means saying so-long to alcohol and hello to lifelong abstinence. It's ironic that their intense reluctance to attend could be seen as a confirmation of their disease. The thought of living without drinking scares the hell out of them.

Does using the term "alcoholic" with a patient do more harm than good?

It might. As we found out from the question about elderly drinkers, the word "alcoholic" virtually crackles with meaning — a bum, a dissolute, the wretched of the earth. I believe the diagnosis of alcoholism may be harmful if applied to one who has this concept and can't give it up; it may also be harmful when applied to an adolescent who is "aggressively experimenting" with alcohol. However, the A-word need only be used in a patient chart. When involved in a Twelve-Step program, it can be substituted for anything that gets the point across. For example, many AA members simply say, "I'm powerless over alcohol" or "I have a desire not to drink today." No one really cares what words are used as long as a person understands his chronic powerlessness over mood-altering chemicals.

How prevalent is alcoholism in the gay community?

One suspects that the number of gays who fit our clinical definition of alcoholism is around 10% (some say as high as 25%). It would not be surprising to discover, however, that a much greater percentage (as high as 60-70%) drink far too much for their health. One reason is that historically, the bar scene has been one of the few places gays could freely socialize. Warning them away from bars, gay or otherwise, is to tell them to trash their social scene as well as put alcohol behind them.

It wouldn't be surprising to find that gays have more trouble preventing relapse than those in so-called "straight" society. Feeling rejected and alone because of their sexual orientation, attending funeral after funeral of loved ones who have died of AIDS — these are among the many factors that would account for this. To prevent relapse, one must be able to "buy into" the future; to have some reason to live. Gays who cannot adjust to the death around them or their status as social outcasts will have a tougher time staying alcohol-free. A thorough bio/psycho/social history, taken at the time of admission, should call attention to sexual orientation so that the treatment needs of any gay or lesbian may be carefully identified and met.

Is there a relationship between alcohol and AIDS?

A person's immune system, even when weakened from the consumption of alcohol and other depressants, does not seem to be much of a factor in becoming infected with HIV. However it does seem to play a major role in staying well once formal HIV diagnosis is made. Many who suffer from full-blown AIDS develop an attitude of "Who cares?" A sober lifestyle, however, will go far toward maintaining quality of life for a person with AIDS.

Does the emotional age of an alcoholic always keep pace with physical age?

Hardly ever. Non-alcoholics (whether they drink socially or maintain abstinence) usually find their emotional maturity keeping pace with their physical maturity. As they make their developmental way from childhood to adolescence and adulthood, they continue to make decisions and take risks — they learn at the school of life, so to speak. They make mistakes, cry a little, nurse a few wounds and then go on. When they become adults, their emotional and physical ages are roughly the same.

Not so with the alcoholic. He always starts down the same path as the non-alcoholic but soon there's a divergence. Whereas the non-alcoholic continues on the somewhat rocky road to maturity, the alcoholic takes off and wanders in the wilderness. None of that wonderfully alliterative "learning life's lessons" for him. When he finally climbs back on the path (if he ever does) he's quick to notice that emotionally speaking, everyone has passed him by. He's as big as everyone else but his maturity level is the same as it was when he started to drink.

Former Senator George McGovern, in his courageous book *Terry*, tells the sad story of his daughter who succumbed to alcoholism at the age of 45. She was found frozen to death in a parking lot near her home in Madison, Wisconsin after many years battling the disease and many trips in and out of public detoxes and treatment centers. McGovern writes that Terry's sister Sue was "startled to hear Terry relating the hurts and wrongs she had suffered within our family — mistreatment by her sisters, insensitivity and neglect on the part of her parents, and the general dysfunctional character of the whole family. As she would relate these family wrongs, her face would fill with anguish and she would begin to weep... She was amazed to discover that

Terry, now twenty-seven, was still speaking as though she were a child."

This is a very articulate and accurate description of the gap that develops between the emotional and physical age of a practicing alcoholic. George McGovern's family noticed that Terry, even at the age of 27, was acting like a child. And why not? She was little more than a child when she began drinking. Through therapy and the practice of a methodical recovery program, it is possible to "catch up," so to speak, with everyone else. But it takes a certain amount of time and isn't it part of the disease that alcoholics want things "right now?"

Is it possible to become an informed helper?

Sure it is. Gerald Egan, in his book *The Skilled Helper*, calls formally-trained psychotherapists, psychologists, therapists, counselors and social workers "First level" helpers. Ministers, rabbis, priests and parents — a so-called "Second level" of helpers — are less trained but are most often the first to know about a problem.

"Third level" helpers (managers, supervisors, hairdressers, etc.) as well as "Fourth level" (friends, acquaintances, relatives and even strangers) may, by learning and practicing certain helping skills, provide a great service to those who are alcoholic or their family and friends.

Such helpers can learn how to act as agents of change; to attend a friend's verbal and non-verbal messages ("active listening"); to identify their own issues and biases; to hold in check their tendency to offer advice; to empathize; to summarize statements; to *bridge* (juxtaposing a friend's statement with another, inconsistent, statement); to *challenge* (juxtaposing a friend's statement with reality); to set realistic goals; model appropriate behavior; explore consequences of behavior and finally, to move the friend toward taking an active part in managing his or her life.

Concerned helpers should also learn so-called "developmental" models — what people are likely to do and say at various ages of development (childhood, adolescence, adulthood, middle age and old age) — in order to distinguish between typical problems of development and more serious social/emotional problems. In other words, what is normal, age-appropriate behavior? In the above question, the sister of Terry McGovern had enough understanding of the developmental model to notice that Terry was physically an adult but emotionally a child.

One skill that will benefit anyone who counsels a friend is learning to recognize the difference between "content" and "process." In therapy-speak, the word *content* means all the details a patient is going to throw at you. And believe me, sometimes it's a blizzard:

"I did this; she did that. Last night she came over with that husband of hers. She said 'That's my toaster.' Well, she can have my car but she'll never get my toaster. That's when that brother of hers came over and got in my face. So I said, 'Oh yeah?'" (For a lyrical and perfectly marvelous example of content see the passage in T. S. Eliot's *The Waste Land*, Pt. II, beginning *When Lil's husband got demobbed...*).

Often, clients get so caught up in content they can't seem to get out of it. Try to sneak in a comment about something of substance — like her obvious anger — and they'll go right back to content; that's their comfort zone.

Process, however, is very different. It's the needle the concerned helper is looking for as he wades through the mighty haystack of content. He's going to listen for this friend's perception of reality. Is she paranoid? Oversensitive to verbal slights? Does she see everything as a personal attack on her? Does the happiness of another seem to diminish hers? Is she a mass of old resentments? Is she dealing with a current crisis or has it brought up "inner child" issues of abandonment that were laid down 40 years ago? Is the person avoiding self-responsibility through passivity (unused human potential), learned helplessness and negative self-talk?

For practice, take an afternoon off and suffer through some of the sensationalistic talk shows like Ricki Lake, Jerry Springer, Montel Williams, et. al. Notice how all the guests barrage their host with so much content that he or she becomes dizzy. With practice, you can learn to sort through all this conscious stuff and truly hear what's in the subconscious of each guest. This is their *process*. And if they don't deal with the dysfunctional way they process relationships, they'll simply go from problem to problem.

Other things to remember as you counsel a friend are:

- Most people don't want to become truly free of emotional pain. That requires a lot of work. They merely want to be more comfortable in their neuroses.
- You must remind your friend that talking to you is not to be construed as taking action on a problem.
- It's important to distinguish feelings from behaviors. "I respect your feelings but I don't respect your behaviors."
- Don't label the feeling of a friend until she labels it first. There's a good chance you will be wrong and it will inadvertently cause her to shut down.
- Unsolicited advice is rarely followed.
- Use your own emotional barometer to "feel" the emotions of your friend.
- When in doubt about a friend's emotions, ask for more information.
- Most people won't work on an issue until enough pain is there to make them ready.
- Don't focus on just your friend; consider all those in her support system.

- People often know what to do about their problems — they just lack the necessary self-esteem or ego-strength to tackle them.
- "Learned helplessness" is a major cause of depression.
- A concerned helper will model problem-solving behaviors.
- Set everything out at the beginning — "You're my friend but I can't fix you."
- You may need to remind your friend that while you respect confidentiality, you also have an obligation (especially if you hear about homicidal or suicidal tendencies or about the physical or sexual abuse of someone under the age of 18) to protect society at large and that may mean alerting authorities.
- Goals must be positive — i.e., they cannot be an *absence* of action.
- Goals must also be behavioral and not constrained by time.
- Goals must be related to the problem or critical to the issue at hand.
- If you do too much for your friend, you might be enabling him to avoid self-responsibility.
- Counseling shouldn't make you tired. If you find that you are working harder than your friend, you're doing it wrong.

If alcoholics relapse because they leave AA, why do they leave AA in the first place?

Newcomers don't seek out an AA meeting because they're happy. No, they do it because something is clearly wrong with their lives. Thus, pain brings people into AA and it should not be surprising that the lack of pain often leads them right back out.

In other words, suppose an alcoholic enters AA after having lost a spouse, children, a home, car, his job and his health. Obviously, he understands that something is wrong. He starts attending meetings, gets a sponsor to guide him and maybe even works the Twelve Steps. Slowly but surely, he gets back his health (always the first to return), his family and his home, he gets his job back and that means a new car is right around the corner. And *voila*, his pain is gone. So why stay in AA? His liver has stopped hurting and he can't even feel his kidneys anymore. But there's just one problem — if he mistakes this good fortune for an ability to handle alcohol, he then goes whistling off to the land of drinking, where, if he's truly an alcoholic, he'll quickly lose all. In other words, the alcoholic has gained power over many other things in his life and can't believe that he hasn't gained power over alcohol. So frequently is this scenario repeated that AA members often wonder whether relapse occurs more often with success than with failure.

Will I pass along alcoholism to my children?

It is clear that alcoholism tends to travel in blood families. If a person has one alcoholic parent, his chances of being alcoholic are high. If a person has two alcoholic parents, his chances are much higher. But it's an inexact science; the genetic influence of alcoholism has been shown to be mitigated by a person's personality. However, if the alcoholic acquaints himself with modern Twelve-Step fundamentals, there's a 100% chance that he may bequeath the legacy of recovery to his children.

I've sat with hundreds of parents of alcoholics many of whom have admitted that, yes, they drank alcoholically in their youth, and yes, they managed to go dry when they married and had children and no, they never found it necessary to mention their drinking problem to their adolescent or adult children. How sad. If they had found the courage to talk about it, they might have confronted a major event in their own lives and their children may have made more informed decisions regarding their consumption of alcohol. But there are thousands of adult children who will never find out that one or both of their biological parents once had a drinking problem. If you are such a parent, please do me a favor and talk to your children about it. Sunlight, Ben Jonson said 400 years ago, is always the best solvent.

Is there an addictive personality?

For decades, people have used the term "addictive personality" as if the phrase were recognized by the mental or behavioral health profession. It is not. To be sure, there are many who seem to fall prey to all forms of addiction. Much like a child's toy which pops up another target when one is hammered down, these people successfully treat one addiction only to succumb to a second or third. They go from alcohol to eating and then, credit card in hand, start addictive shopping. But labeling someone's personality as addictive is an after-the-fact deduction showing ignorance about the complexity of the human personality.

Ironically, it seems that recovering alcoholics are the quickest to use the term. They'll say, "Well, that's just my addictive personality coming out." "You know us alcoholics — we're just sicker than others." To hear them tell it, so-called "earth people" (non-alcoholics) aren't the least bit impatient, insecure, devious, disingenuous, cunning, two-faced, prey to easy solutions or quick to lie.

Where ex-drunks got the idea that they're "lowlier than thou" or have most of the world's character defects is anybody's guess. Perhaps it has to do with untreated egotism. Yes, AA members, to reduce their stress, therapeutically discuss their fear, anger and lack of patience. But it doesn't mean they've cornered the market on them.

Is it possible to become addicted to AA meetings?

True recovery is where an alcoholic attends the daily or weekly AA meetings he needs and spends the rest of the week practicing what he learns in the meetings. If, however, he merely "hides out" from life in meetings (just as he hid out from life in a bar), he's attending them for the wrong reason. That will interfere with his life as surely as addictive drinking will. A person who attends AA for the wrong reason could be thought of as addicted only if he needed outside help to stop attending.

Am I personally optimistic about what the millennium holds for alcoholism?

I am certainly optimistic about the ability of alcoholics and their loved ones to recover in treatment and in Twelve-Step groups. However, I'm less than optimistic about what the 21st century holds for the disease itself. I see it going like this:

Congress and the US Supreme Court will continue to express skepticism as to the effectiveness of alcoholism treatment while continuing to see alcoholism as a self-induced malady. State legislatures will cautiously revise downward their legal definition of intoxication from .10 to .08. This will undoubtedly snare some of their own members and the legal definition will go back up.

Society will continue to yearn for a time when the sin model of alcoholism carried the day. It will fund treatment for those already in the criminal justice system but will be parsimonious about funds for the non-criminal population. Fundamentalist and charismatic religions, caught napping during the behavioral health heyday of the 70s and 80s, will establish their own treatment centers where alcoholism will be seen as a Satan-inspired lack of commitment to their own brand of piety. Most people will ignore the warning of author Susan Sontag and continue to see alcoholism (and AIDS) as a metaphor for a declining and Godless civilization.

Community-based counseling agencies such as the NCADD system will receive financial shortfalls from local United Ways facing intense pressure to financially support environmental groups and ethnic minorities. Public detox centers will pay the price for their success in removing public inebriates by being abandoned by politicians who opt for cheaper outpatient detox centers. Voters will then notice a return of the public inebriates and vow that something must be done.

Private industry, under the guise of competition with the Japanese, will continue to tread the road of a false economy by getting rid of Employee Assistance Programs. News programs like *60 Minutes* will continue to tout the so-called health benefits of wine until they're asked to quit by the medical profession which notices a distinct under-reporting of adverse health consequences.

The beer, wine and distilled spirits industry will initially react to the tobacco industry lawsuits like an unsuspecting football coach reacts to being doused with an ice-cold tub of Gatorade. Appropriately chastened, they will stop the marketing of beer and so-called "alcopops" to underage kids — at least until the heat's off.

Comedy routines reminiscent of Dean Martin, Foster Brooks and Cheech & Chong will decline as society continues to find drunks, impaired drivers and drug-addled public transportation operators not the least bit funny.

Scientific research will provide further proof that alcoholism has strong biological and genetic links. Behaviorists will continue to ignore 70 years of alcohol treatment history and once again attempt to prove that alcoholics can learn to drink socially if they just use a little willpower! Many books will be sold in this attempt and many lives will be lost. The American health care industry, which spends 60% of its money on the last two years of a person's life, will continue to ignore the wellness movement and its campaign for disease prevention.

Mountebanks and nostrum peddlers will continue to offer "microwave sobriety" wherein two days is all it takes to CURE YOUR ALCOHOLISM!!! Sadly, they'll make a lot of money and do a lot of damage. Russia will continue to take note of the damage alcoholism is doing to their people and look to America and its treatment/support group models for help. And finally, no one will bother to take late therapist Viktor Frankl's sage advice to complement the Statue of Liberty on the East Coast with a Statue of *Responsibility* on the West Coast.

What's the hardest addiction to quit?

The last one. By that I mean the *final* one. All too often, persons recovering from one addiction develop another one. The alcoholic, for instance, prides himself on not drinking but slowly begins to substitute eating for alcohol. He medicates feelings with it, hides it, uses it to avoid intimacy and considers it a well-earned reward. Or perhaps the recovering alcoholic begins to shop her troubles away and soon finds herself with a deck of maxed-out credit cards. This is the vanity of switching addictions as surely as if the alcoholic went from gin to Scotch or from beer to marijuana. The result is always the same — guilt, frustration, social, financial and legal problems.

The insightful alcoholic (and his loved ones) must finally come to terms with the idea that there's nothing from the outside that can be placed inside to fix him. He simply cannot drink, eat, accumulate, snort, shoot, insert, drop, shove, skin-pop, slam, smoke, huff, marry, buy, or bet on anything that will give him serenity. Serenity is an inside job. It doesn't come from a can, a bottle, a tub of ice cream, a hypodermic needle, a dog track, a slot machine, the bathroom scales, the New York Stock Exchange, the top of Mt. Everest, a wedding chapel, the end of a bungie cord or the shoe department at Nordstrom's. When that final addiction goes, the alcoholic has nothing to fall back on but Twelve-Step support groups to help him make profound behavioral changes. Sooner or later, the alcoholic must work on him or herself.

Epilogue

It bears repeating that talking to someone about a problem is not taking action on that problem.

Neither is reading a book.

It's wisdom to remember that understanding is a consequence of action; not the other way around.

Taking action on a problem as complex as alcoholism is risky. You often must summon all the courage you can muster. Courage to shun your isolation, to meet new people, to share secrets, to seek answers — courage, in short, to do something with the knowledge you've just gained.

In the *Introduction*, I stated that you cannot simply read this or any other book and get someone sober. The proper course of action upon finishing this book is to pick up that 50-pound telephone and make a call to the National Council on Alcoholism and Drug Dependence at 212-206-6770. They'll direct you to a local affiliate and there you'll discover compassion, care and understanding.

Jellinek V-Chart
(read from left to right)

EARLY STAGE

- Increased tolerance
- Sneaks drinks
- Avoids talking about drinking
- Preoccupation with alcohol
- Can't stop drinking when others do
- Occasional relief drinking
- Memory blackouts begin (in some persons)
- Increasing alcohol dependence
- Family is concerned/complains
- Feelings of guilt
- Loss of control
- Alibis for drinking
- Feels remorse

MIDDLE STAGE

- Extravagant/aggressive behavior
- Family is more worried, angry
- Swears off
- Efforts at control fail over and over
- Hides alcohol supply
- Promises fail
- Avoids family and friends
- Work/money troubles
- Tremors/early morning drinking
- Protects supply
- Decrease in tolerance
- Drinks with inferiors
- Vague spiritual desires
- Collapse of alibi system
- Admits complete defeat
- Makes late night phone calls
- Tries geographical escape
- Loses other interests
- Memory blackouts increase
- Unreasonable resentments
- Neglects food
- Physical deterioration
- Impaired thinking
- Indefinable fears
- Obsesses about drinking
- Ethics deteriorate

END STAGE

- Obsessive drinking continues in vicious circles
- Stops drinking

RECOVERY

- Has honest desire for help
- Learns alcoholism is an illness
- Told addiction can be stopped
- Meets happy and sober alcoholics
- Begins right thinking
- Takes care of self physically
- Appreciates possibilities of new way of life
- Better eating habits
- Realistic thinking
- Family and friends appreciate efforts
- New circle of friends
- Courage to face facts
- Increased emotional control
- Employers more confident
- Starts group therapy
- Guilt feelings lessen
- Examines spiritual needs
- Takes care of appearance
- Fears diminish
- Self-esteem returns
- Has no more desire to escape
- Adjusts to family's needs
- Develops new interests
- Has ideals again
- Appreciates real values
- Handles money better
- Continues group therapy and mutual help
- Enjoys life at higher level than ever before
- Contented in sobriety
- Appreciates spiritual values

Glossary

abstinence
A total cessation of the use of beverage alcohol. This is maintained by working a methodical recovery program that continuously reminds the alcoholic that he is (and will remain) powerless over alcohol (contrast with *temperance*).

addiction
An addict is a person with a pathological problem who, once he or she chooses to start something, finds it extremely difficult to stop. An addiction always involves a physical drug or a harmful activity which provides the same arousal or tranquilizing effect of a drug (food, shopping, gambling, etc.) Alcoholics, for instance, often act against their own wishes ("I really want to drink but I know I shouldn't.") but their consumption of the first drink is always a conscious choice (contrast with *compulsion*).

affect
(Pronounced <u>AF</u>-fect) A wide range of observable mental processes having to do with feelings or emotions — euphoria, anger, sadness, etc. (contrast with *cognitive*).

cognitive
The forms of "knowing;" this includes perceiving, imagining, reasoning, beliefs and judging (contrast with *affect*).

compulsion

A mostly-subconscious behavior where a person acts totally against his or her own will (non-stop talking, repeated hand washing, etc.). There's no drug or drug-like agent involved and the person engaged in the compulsive behavior gets no euphoria or "payoff" from it (contrast with *addiction*).

confrontation

Generally, an ill-thought out attempt to sway an alcoholic into abstinence or moderation(!). Confrontations don't work, have a detrimental effect on the alcoholic and can be dangerous to all. Confrontations, which have been largely replaced by formal interventions, fail to work in part because they allow the alcoholic's enabling system to remain in place.

content

Any conscious material (words, arguments, descriptions, postures or reactions) provided to a therapist by another. A therapist must listen to or observe a patient's content closely for a glimpse of how he subconsciously relates to other individuals or groups of individuals (his *process*).

ego defenses

Sigmund Freud was first to describe ego defense mechanisms which are relatively involuntary patterns of feelings, thoughts or behaviors used to cope with anxiety and protect the ego. Most are normal adaptive behaviors which become harmful only when used to avoid facing reality. Among the defenses typically used by alcoholics are: *Projection*: blaming others for the alcoholic's problems; *Denial*: distorting reality (that is apparent to others) by refusing to believe that a drinking problem exists; *Rationalization*: finding a rational reason for an irrational act; *Identification*: done in a negative manner by the alcoholic who searches out inferiors with whom he can feel at home when drinking; *Compensation*:

trying to use positive traits to compensate for negative traits such as alcoholism. For example, alcoholics often compensate for their disease by becoming overly helpful to family and neighbors; *Undoing*: the symbolic attempt to make amends or "undo" guilt for previous thoughts, feelings or actions. For instance, the alcoholic will often purchase lavish gifts for a child or spouse who is ignored during drinking bouts.

enabler

A person, family, institution or any system that, in the mistaken belief they are helping an alcoholic, actually hinders or obstructs his recovery. Enablers do for the alcoholic what he should be doing for himself. By providing him with material goods or creature comforts, enablers prevent the alcoholic from finding a personal level of pain sufficient to motivate his entry into recovery. Recovery often starts for all when each enabler becomes aware of her powerlessness over an alcoholic, begins to focus on her own needs and starts a recovery program in Al-Anon Family Groups.

enabling system

An aggregate of persons (family or otherwise) and/or institutions which provide undesirable support to an alcoholic to the extent that he fails to understand that his drinking has consequences. Such a system might include an employer, co-workers, church or synagogue, service club or sports team.

formal intervention

A methodical and disciplined process which brings an alcoholic face-to-face with the consequences of his drinking so that help may be sought. Often done by family members, formal interventions work because they collapse the enabling system of the alcoholic leaving him with no realistic option other than seeking help.

half-life
The half-life of a drug is the amount of time it takes for the body to eliminate half of the drug from the bloodstream. The half-life of beverage alcohol is quite short making its detoxification abrupt and often fatal. The half-life of such benzodiazapines as Valium is 20-50 hours making its detoxification a long and painful experience.

insidiousness
The way in which a harmful agent such as alcohol impairs spiritual, mental, emotional and physical health with such stealth and slowness that an impaired person scarcely knows how sick he is becoming.

intervention
Any activity, planned or otherwise, that results in an alcoholic understanding the consequences of his drinking. Interventions may be social, legal (DUI), medical or psychiatric (see *formal intervention*).

managed care
In response to the high cost of medical care, a system of Managed Health Care was developed in the 1980s which strove to make health care affordable. While Managed Care has helped hold the line on medical costs, it is seen by many as "managed cost," an unfeeling system which adds a layer of administration between the doctor and his or her patient, thereby removing medical decisions from the physician and changing his or her status from management to labor.

milieu therapy
A form of alcoholism treatment which, by providing activities, consistency, structure and discipline on a daily basis, attempts to foster positive habits, thoughts, behaviors and support systems.

process

1. The way in which a person comes to understand or act upon relationships or external reality. A person's "process" is largely subconscious; it is not the "content" of what they say, but "why" and "how" they say it; it is not what they hear but "why" and "how" they hear it. For instance, a person, alcoholic or otherwise, might perceive friendly advice as uncalled-for criticism.

2. The way in which a change in a person's thinking or behavior is brought about (contrast with *content*).

process group

A therapist-led circle of persons attempting to discover why, as individuals, they seem to distort external reality and experience difficulty with relationships. The focus of such a group is not the "content" of what each person says, but "how" and "why" they say it.

recovery

A system of choices made on a continuous basis to refrain from behaviors yielding negative results in favor of those that yield positive results. Recovery must be methodical, progressive and sustained; it is best done in groups of like-minded persons who provide support and encouragement. Recovery does not mean a lack of problems; it means choosing to practice recovery principles during any and all problems. Recovery often means a total overhaul of one's physical, emotional, mental and spiritual life.

relapse

A return to the use of beverage alcohol by an alcoholic. Relapse is a process in which the alcoholic fails to take his disease seriously and thereby falls victim to a complex system of emotional, mental and spiritual stresses which are temporarily relieved by alcohol. Relapse may be a positive experience if it confirms to the alcoholic his powerlessness over alcohol. *Note*: the word *recidivism* should not be used as a synonym for relapse. Recidivism is a criminal justice word that when used in a behavioral health sense, criminalizes the alcoholic.

reverse tolerance
A sign of major liver damage. Tolerance (a classic symptom of alcoholism) means the need for more of the same chemical to achieve the same high. *Reverse* tolerance, however, occurs when the alcoholic has drunk so much alcohol that he suffers hardening or scarring of the liver (cirrhosis). When this happens, the alcoholic appears to get drunk on a very small quantity of alcohol.

social drinker
A person who consumes alcohol only in the context of food or a social/religious occasion. A person who doesn't drink solely for effect. Social drinkers are never surprised by what they do when they drink; they do not exhibit tolerance or any other classic symptom of alcoholism.

temperance
Prior to the development of the disease aspect of alcoholism in the 1930s, it was thought that alcoholics could learn to moderate their drinking; i.e., to drink without getting drunk or causing problems. This was called temperance. Today, however, it is clear that alcoholics are constitutionally incapable of moderating their drinking. Thus, temperance has fallen from favor and has been replaced by abstinence (see *abstinence*).

twelve-step group
Alcoholics Anonymous and its offspring (Al-Anon, Narcotics Anonymous, Cocaine Anonymous, etc.) have as their foundation the idea that incorporating twelve time-proven suggestions will benefit recovery. The Twelve Steps are de-

signed to shatter the illusion of control, enhance spirituality, admit personal responsibility for actions done while drunk or sober, rectify past wrongs and essentially replace the stress of life with serenity. Filling a recovering person with the richness of a life based on Twelve-Step principles greatly reduces the spiritual vacuum which alcohol may have been used to fill.

Suggested Reading

General Reading

de Saint-Exupery, Antoine. 1971. *The Little Prince*. Harcourt Brace & Company.

McGovern, George. 1996. *Terry*. Villard Books.

Egan, Gerard. 1997. *The Skilled Helper*. Brooks/Cole Publishing Company.

Laing, R.D. 1967. *The Politics of Experience*. Random House, Inc.

Sontag, Susan. 1990. *Illness as Metaphor and AIDS and Its Metaphors*. Anchor Books.

Formal Interventions

Johnson, Vernon E. 1986. *Intervention: How to Help Someone Who Doesn't Want Help*. Johnson Institute Books.

Assertiveness Techniques & I-Statements

Alberti, Robert E. and Emmons, Michael. 1995. *Your Perfect Right*. Impact Publishing.

Codependency

Beattie, Melody. 1996. *Codependent No More*. Hazelden Books.

Stages of Grief

Kubler-Ross, Elisabeth. 1997. *On Death and Dying*. Anchor Books.

Alcoholism's Impact on the Family

Wegscheider-Cruse, Sharon. 1989. *Another Chance: Hope and Health for the Alcoholic Family.* Science and Behavior Books.

WEBSITE Information

ncadd.org for the National Council on Alcoholism & Drug Dependence/New York.

asam.org for the American Society of Addiction Medicine/New York.

aa.org for Alcoholics Anonymous.

al-anon-alateen.org for Al-Anon Family Groups and Alateen.

health.org for the National Clearinghouse for Alcohol and Drug Information.

WEBSITE Treatment

valleyhope.com for Valley Hope Treatment Centers (Kansas, Missouri, Nebraska, Oklahoma, Colorado and Arizona).

hazelden.org for Hazelden Foundation of Center City, Minnesota.

bettyfordcenter.org for The Betty Ford Center of Rancho Mirage, California.

Index

About the Author

Kenneth Lucas is a certified counselor and marketing director for Valley Hope Association of Chandler/Tempe, Arizona. He also volunteers as a co-facilitator of The Many Faces of Chemical Dependency drop-in group at the Franciscan Renewal Center of Paradise Valley. In 1996, he was certified as an interventionist by The Johnson Institute. He is a former journalist and has been a CD counselor since 1988. From 1989 to 1996, he was administrator/counselor for NCADD/Phoenix where he provided informational programs for the general public. This responsibility, coupled with his NCADD counseling duties, gave him the impetus to write this book.

Lucas is a native of Wichita, Kansas and lives in Phoenix with wife, graphic designer Pat Kenny.